AXIS OF WEASELS

By Bill Schmalfeldt

Published by Radio Wiseguys
2014

© 2014 by Bill Schmalfeldt

First Printing: 2014

ISBN: 1499637187

ISBN-13: 978-1499637182

I0482845

Dedication

I have friends who have stood by me through this whole ordeal. They would probably rather not be mentioned. They know who they are. My stalwart sister in Milwaukee, far tougher than I ever was and I ever will be. I love ya, Bexter, with all my heart.

Raven and Shiloh, it's not time to go outside yet. Mom will tell you when it is time. Stop barking at the garbage man. They are not stealing our garbage. Please be quiet.

Gail. You are my life. Is there anything more I can say than that? I am lost without you. I know this whole thing has made you as angry at me as I am at the shitheels who caused this suffering. But I love you, I thank you, I depend on you, and I can not countenance the thought of life without you.

Foreword

In May 2012, while keeping myself busy post retirement after Parkinson's disease robbed me of my ability to handle the daily commute from home to work, I became interested in a story about a young Republican operative who had achieved levels of success that seemed remarkable for someone with his limited education and challenging background. I learned that he was the front man for an organization calling itself the National Bloggers Club, Inc., and that it had been created as a fund-raising operation to assist a blogger named Aaron Worthing who claimed to have lost his job as a result of being "terrorized" by a man named Brett Kimberlin – known for being convicted as "The Speedway Bomber" in suburban Indianapolis in the late 1970s. That part of the story didn't interest me as much as the fact that this obviously partisan organization was claiming a 501(c)3 tax exempt status with the IRS, meaning that people donating to the organization could claim their donation as a tax deduction. I contacted the CEO, as I had done with dozens of non-profit CEOs over my years as a journalist, and asked for the proof that a non-profit is required to present upon request.

The door was opened, and I stepped through it of my own accord, not noticing the sign atop the archway…

"Abandon All Hope All Ye Who Enter Here."

Preface

It has always seemed strange to me... the things we admire in men, kindness and generosity, openness, honesty, understanding and feeling, are the concomitants of failure in our system. And those traits we detest, sharpness, greed, acquisitiveness, meanness, egotism and self-interest, are the traits of success. And while men admire the quality of the first they love the produce of the second.

-- John Steinbeck

Honesty is for the most part less profitable than dishonesty.

-- Plato

You know, there's nothing you can do about your public image. It is what it is. I just try to do things honestly. I guess honesty is what you would call subjective: if you feel good about what you're doing, yourself, if you figure you're doing the right thing.

-- Christopher Walken

Histories are more full of examples of the fidelity of dogs than of friends.

-- Alexander Pope

Introduction

Reputation is an idle and most false imposition; oft got without merit, and lost without deserving.

--William Shakespeare

I took a great deal of care to develop a reputation that would serve me well as a legacy. I've had my failures as a man and as a human being. But when the balance is weighed and weighed honestly, I believe when all is said and done the world will be seen to have been a better place for my being in it.

I served two hitches in the US Navy. I've been in all 50 states. I was a Navy corpsman as part of a Marine Amphibous Unit that evacuated the American Embassy in Beirut in 1976. I lived in Japan for 18 months. I've been married to the woman of my dreams since 1989. When diagnosed with Parkinson's disease in 2000, I immediately began looking for ways to advocate for new and better treatments for this progressive neurological disorder. In 2007, I participated in a Clinical Trial at Vanderbilt University to see whether or not folks in the earlier stages of Parkinson's could survive deep brain stimulation surgery and then tolerate the implantation of the hardware on a long-term basis. Since retiring from my job at the National Institutes of Health in 2011, I've written about my life, I've written liberal satire, I've written investigative journalism pieces. I am not proud of everything I've done in my life. But all in all, I think God will find me to be a good and faithful servant when my time comes.

I don't surprise easily. But I am startled, shocked and dismayed by the level of hatred exhibited by a gang of right wing lunatics who have made my destruction their personal business for reasons you will read in this book.

I got an e-mail from a friend of mine today. He said…

I have never seen anyone get so under someone else's skin like (you did). I need to try and figure out just what method you used to light their asses on fire and make a playbook out of it. Seriously, these guys are literally on fire when it comes to you. BK? They hardly even comment about him. Bill? They got 200 comments on each minor post. Jeez Louise, wtf.. I never seen such hate all balled up into one guy who is disabled and can't hardly get out of the house.

I was shocked, and remain dismayed over the sheer level of gleeful hate exhibited by the right wing fans of minor-league blogger William John Joseph Hoge III.

Death threats. Vile, obscene emails. Using images of my dead mother as avatars. Disgusting, horrible language directed at a person they have never met and do not know, other than the descriptions they have read about me from the blog of Mr. Hoge.

They will tell you that their hatred from me is justified because I am a horrible person, a liar, an adjudicated cyberstalker. But their entire body of knowledge about me is filtered through what they "know" about me from Hoge, from right wingers Ali Akbar, R. Stacy McCain, Lee Stranahan and the people who follow them like drooling sycophants, waiting for each word, scouring through my writing, looking for things to be outraged over.

Parkinson's disease is not a fatal condition. You die with it, not of it. Hoge knew I had Parkinson's when he filed the first of his 367 criminal charges against me. That is not a misprint. Three Hundred Sixty Seven criminal charges.

Bloggers like Hoge, McCain and others have trashed my reputation. Where three years ago, a Google Search of my last name would turn up links to my writing about Parkinson's disease, my books written to raise money for research, my blogs of liberal satire and the like.

That same Google Search today will show me to be a "deranged cyberstalker" with an "anal rape fetish" who "torments dead babies."

There's nothing I can do about that. I've been ruined. I am unable to find paying work as a freelance writer because who wants a dead baby tormentor on the masthead?

All I can do is tell my story.

I tried this four times previously. Twice my books were throttled in their cribs by WJJ Hoge who does not want this story to be told. Once, an individual falsely claimed ownership of a picture he did not actually own. The fourth time, a woman claimed ownership of a photo she does not own. These people would much rather lay me in my grave, sooner rather than later, with the reputation THEY helped create for me, not for what I've actually done in my life.

Bill Schmalfeldt
May 21, 2014

Chapter 1 - I HAVE FRIENDS!

I have friends who are concerned about me. But not so nearly concerned as my enemies. Today is April 24, 2014. Yesterday, two very kind police officers were dispatched to my house to check to see if I was inclined to injure myself.

This happened last summer as well.

I realize how crazy this sounds. But remember. Just because you may be paranoid doesn't really mean someone isn't out to get you. We'll talk more about that later.

The nice officers wouldn't tell me who alerted them to my impending suicide. They didn't have to. I know who called them.

My friends who are concerned about me are trying to deal with the main bully who has been attacking this 59-year old man who lives with his wife, his stepson and two overly-entitled dogs for no other reason than this man who needs assistance to walk, who hurt his right arm this morning trying to lift himself from his office chair, this very dangerous, nearly immobile, profoundly handicapped man in his 15th year with Parkinson's disease, dared to write about him.

My friends who are concerned about me have asked me to remain quiet about the bullying on Twitter while they try to form some plan of action. I have honored this request. I have been nothing but friendly and pleasant on Twitter. That very fact is a subject of mockery by the people who comment on the Hogewash.com blog. The people who are knowingly using my Parkinson's disease to cause my early death or total disability. When I'm quiet, when I don't provide grist for their mill, it makes them angry.

As you will see, the main antagonist in this story has a restraining order against me. Today, on his blog, he is alleging that I have contacted him in direct violation of the order. I have not. But he has proof!

And, as I sit here, being quiet, being nice, being friendly, being GOOD, I see that one of these cretins, a familiar at the Hogewash.com blog who calls himself Paul Krendler after the "Hannibal" character played by Ray Liotta in the "Silence of the Lamb" sequel, has penned a witty "satire" about me.

It starts on the next page. I had to summarize and paraphrase it. You see, "Paul Krendler" is ashamed of what he wrote. He doesn't want you to see it, unless you are already convinced that Bill Schmalfeldt is a disgusting piece of slime.

He couldn't challenge the copyright without revealing his true identity. He was contacted by WJJ Hoge, who killed a previous edition of this book using methods I will reveal after you read this paraphrased summary.

On the first page of the blog, the rights to which were allegedly purchased by WJJ Hoge of Westminster, Maryland, the writer, "Paul Krendler" mentions me by name, calls me old, crazy, fat and demented.

He writes that my wife, who he also names, is rarely home at night, spending that time wandering the streets in the city in which I live, which he also names, to get away from "the unrelented stink of old diapers and sweating feet." He writes that she spends her days sleeping off the hangover from her all night drinking. Neither my wife nor I are drinkers... her by choice, me because alcohol mixed with my medications would make me dead.

He also mocks the journalism awards I've received over my more than 30 years in the business. Oh, yes. I also have mayonanaise all over my fists.

On the second page of the Hoge-acquired material, "Krendler" mocks my late identical twin brother, Bob, who died in 2004. He creates a sick scenario in which I have fond memories of having sex with my late twin brother.

The door bangs open. It's my wife, home from her night of drinking.

He describes her as wearing a long, Army surplus winter coat, thereby making it impossible for me to see whether or not she had lost yet another skirt during the night.

It is 10:30 in the morning in "Krendler's" scenario and my wife is still drunk and screeching at me.

In her hand, she clutches a nearly empty fifth of bourbon.

The third page of the material Hoge claims he "owns" starts with a depiction of my wife standing there with her panties dangling around her left ankle.

She leaves, but not before issuing a wet-sounding fart that rattles the awards on my wall.

My wife passes out on her bed without getting undressed, and "Krendler" imagines me hoping she will not urinate in the bed -- again.

He writes of my despair at nobody purchasing any of my writing or donating to my Pay Pal account.

The only people who comment on my blog are... me, according to "Krendler's" telling of this sordid tale.

There are seven more pages, all much like the first three, in which "Krendler" depicts me as moaning over a failed life, more sexual fantasies about my dead twin brother and me (involving foot-long hot dogs, yet).

He finds time to mock my Parkinson's disease, the fact that I am in the early stages of Parkinson's disease dementia. "Krendler" refers to the person who he "sold" the "rights" to this blog, WJJ Hoge of Westminster, Maryland, and the fact that he has filed 367 unfounded criminal charges against me, all of which were dismissed. But the harassment I experience is all in my mind. One last description of my wife having a "freakishly large head", followed by mockery of my being in a wheelchair, my relationship with my kids, a charming image of my wife vomiting in the toilet...

And, scene....

And there we have it. A condensed version of the 10 pages of 14-point copy that was included in my original telling of this story.

The intention, of course, was to show you, the reader unaware that such evil exists in the world, the lengths and depths a megalomanic will go to in order to keep the world from reading his victim's account of the 15-month onslaught that has left his victim a physical shadow of his former self.

This man, this WJJ Hoge possesses an evil craftiness. Aware that as of this writing there is more than a month left on his ill-gotten "peace order," he was aware that he was the only person in the world who could submit a DMCA takedown claim to the publisher of the original book, and make it stick – not because of the merits of his claim, of which there are none, but because the peace order makes it impossible for me to contact him to discuss the terms of his "ownership" of this material, how he came to own it, and to ask for proof that he actually does own it.

CreateSpace, Amazon and other self-publishing houses are not in the "art" business. They are not in the "truth" business. They are in the business of selling stuff and not getting sued while selling it.

That explains how Hoge was able to throttle the initial iteration of "Intentional Infliction" – an e-book called "My Slow, Journalistic Death."

In that book, I made the mistake of copying and pasting a single sentence from Hoge's actual blog. He filed a copyright complaint with "Smashwords", the company that published the e-book, and the company folded faster than Superman on laundry day.

When CreateSpace notified me it was suspending availability of "Intentional Infliction," they made it clear they would be happy to put it back on the shelves as soon as Mr. Hoge and I could come to terms on an agreement for me to use "his material" in "my book." I explained that was, in fact, impossible as my contacting Hoge would be a violation of the Maryland Peace Order laws. CreateSpace had no choice in the matter. (See the paragraph about what business they are in.) and the book was effectively killed. Before its untimely death, it was savagely attacked on the book's Amazon page. Frequent readers of Hoge's blog who had Amazon accounts wrote 1-star reviews of the book, without benefit of having purchased or even read the thing.

Some went so far as to go back and offer 1-star reviews of books I wrote as long as 10-years ago, including my book about my experience as a volunteer for brain surgery, told in my book "Put On Your Parky Face" (available at my home page, www.radiowiseguy.com if you're interested.)

What Hoge and his minions fail to realize, time after time, attack after attack, is this.

They haven't killed me. Not yet.

Yes, the constant threat of jail occasioned by having 367 criminal charges hanging over my head did a number on the progression of my Parkinson's disease. It is a settled fact that increased levels of stress cause the natural progression of Parkinson's disease to proceed at an even faster rate. This is a fact known to Hoge. It is his ultimate desire, in my opinion, to use my own brain as a murder weapon – to cause my death or total disability by piling on as much stress as possible while chuckling like a giant, fat spider in its web, watching as the fly struggles to free itself.

I thought I was free of WJJ Hoge when he was finally granted "his Precioussssssss…." The thing I believe he values more than his wife and his mountainous manchild. (Shame that the proud WJJ Hoge lineage will end at IV, but it is what it is.)

On his third try, he was finally granted… a peace order!

Chapter 2 – GOLDEN MEMORIES

The petitioner sat at his table in the Carroll County, Maryland, Circuit Court room, his hands folded beneath his beard, a smug look of assurance on his face. This was his third shot at getting a peace order – known in most states as a restraining order – against the respondent. He had been rejected twice at the District Court level. This time, there was reason for the confident look on his face. This time he had a lawyer.

Zoa Barnes, attorney at law. The very smart and capable attorney, sister-in-law of the Carroll County State's Attorney, Jerry Barnes, was arguing the petitioner's case. The respondent sat on the left hand side of the judge, accused of using the social media platform "Twitter" to harass her client by using "at mentions" (a Twitter device whereby one can mention a person by placing an "@" in front of another person's user name, at mentions are utilized to let the sender's readers know that the sender is writing about a specific person. Even if the specific person is not "following" the sender's account, an "at mention" will show up on that person's "notifications" page – unless the person being "at mentioned" has "blocked" the sender.)

Ms. Barnes had just finished explaining to the Honorable Judge Thomas Stansfield of the Carroll County Circuit Court that "blocking" the respondent's Twitter account would be the same thing as the petitioner having to change his telephone number to avoid telemarketers. She argued that her client should not be forced to disable a portion of his Internet accessibility just to block someone on Twitter.

The respondent's lawyer, seeming to recognize Ms. Barnes' argument as twaddle meant to confuse a "luddite" judge, argued that case after case, precedent after precedent, in state and federal courts, showed that Twitter was nothing more than a bulletin board where random people post random thoughts and ideas, and that as a reader of that bulletin board, Ms. Barnes' client had the choice to read or ignore whatever was tacked to that bulletin board by the respondent.

Judge Stansfield listened to both sides, in as much as the word "listen" means the reception of sound into the inner ear, the electrical impulses are sent to the brain and interpreted as words. But his mind was made up.

His Honor told the court that he had no idea what "The Twitter" was, what it was for, how to use it, or whatever, but if that nice old man at the petitioner table wanted to be left alone, then by cracky, he had the right to be left alone.

He found for the petitioner and instituted a six month peace order. At the end of the six months, the petitioner with the same lawyer who was the same sister-in-law of the same county State's Attorney made the same argument to the same judge and the peace order was extended for another six months, despite the respondent's Power Point presentation of how one expert after another has gone on record as saying Twitter is not a platform for direct contact. It is a broadcast platform. All the petitioner had to do was block the respondent's Twitter feed, and he would never have to read another word the respondent wrote. The petitioner argued that he wanted to be able to read the respondent's Twitter feed anytime the mood struck him. He just didn't want the respondent using the "@" symbol in front of his name.

That made sense to the judge, who sat on the bench with a guilty and sad look on his face, twisting a rubber band absent-mindedly as he pronounced that there was good cause to extend the peace order for another six months.

Therefore, until June 14, 2014, the respondent is forbidden to "commit or threaten to commit any of the following acts against the petitioner: an act which causes serious bodily harm; an act that places the petitioner in fear of imminent serious bodily harm; assault, rape, attempted rape, sexual offense, or attempted sexual offense; false imprisonment; harassment; stalking; trespass; or malicious destruction of property. The respondent shall not contact (in person, by telephone, in writing, or by any other means), attempt to contact or harass the petitioner. The respondent shall not enter the residence of the petitioner, including yard, grounds, outbuildings and common areas surrounding the dwelling.

The peace order places a lot of restrictions on the person serving under the order. It places no restrictions on the person holding the order.

In this case, less than a month after being awarded the original peace order, the petitioner attempted to "follow" the respondent's Twitter feed. The respondent rejected the request. But the petitioner would not be ignored so easily.

After writing hundreds of posts on his blog that mention the respondent by name after being awarded the peace order, after filing 367 misdemeanor criminal charges against the respondent for "violating" the peace order – of which all 367 were dismissed by the State's Attorneys of Carroll and Howard County, the petition has found a new way to provoke the respondent.

This book is a result of that harassment.

Chapter 3 – HOGE GETS HIS 'PRECIOUSSSSS…'

According to the online biography on his aptly named "hogewash.com" blog, William John Joseph Hoge III was born on New Year's Eve, 1946-47 – ostensibly to William John Joseph Hoge II. The glorious nativity took place in Nashville, although there was no star in the sky to herald the arrival of the man who would later claim full control of the author's life.

After graduating from Vanderbilt University with a degree in electrical engineering, he joined the Army. By the mid 1970s, Hoge was taking credit for product innovations in consumer audio, professional sound and musical instrument products. He retired from his position as a contract engineer at the Goddard Space Flight Center in 2013 before his various legal battles, we assume, caused him to come out of retirement at age 67 to pay for his habit of trying to destroy peoples' lives in various courts of law.

Hoge claims to be the founding Chairman of the Nashville Section of the Audo Engineering Society, and he has published a number of articles in the various geek journals favored by folks who like that sort of thing.

Hoge fancies himself a minister of some sort at a Westminster, Maryland, church that has no home building, whose members take turns holding meeting of what must be a tiny congregation.

The author's personal impressions of Hoge are consistent with the kind of little old man who sits in the back row of every city council meeting in every small town in America who objects every time the city government seeks to raise revenue for street or sewer repair.

For someone who came to play such an important part in the author's life by the end of 2013, in late 2012 I had only a vague knowledge that he even existed, although by then I had already allegedly invaded the computer server of some server farm in Kansas City and used it to send abusive comments to Hoge.

As I've written, I have Parkinson's disease. I am retired from the federal government, where I was employed as a writer-editor because of the advance of his disease, a fact known to Hoge and his confederates who the reader will get to know later in the narrative.

Anyhoo…

I was vaguely aware of Hoge's existence as an oxygen user on the face of the planet by the end of 2012. He had referred to me in his blog when I threatened to sue another individual, Aaron Walker of Manassas, Virginia, for claiming that I had leveled a rape threat against the family of another individual, Lee Stranahan of Dallas.

The first time of the thousands of times Hoge mentioned me in his blog was on September 3, 2012, when he wrote that I was "some bozo calling himself the Liberal Grouch," who appeared to be a member of Brett Kimberlin's "clown posse" and that I was threatening to sue Aaron Walker for defamation.

(I could take up several hundred pages explaining thewhole Brett Kimberlin story, but I will spare the reader other than to say Kimberlin is currently suing Hoge, Walker and several other people on a variety of charges in state and federal court for defamation, libel, intentional infliction of emotional distress, stalking, harassment, and several civil racketeering charges. Look it up.)

Hoge used his first mention of me in his "hogewash" blog to raise money, saying that if I was "stupid enough" to sue Walker, he would be the first in line to make "a substantial donation" to the Blogger Defense Team to help pay Walker's expenses.

After reading this, I used the contact form on the blog and asked Hoge to at least consider my side of the story before calling me names and taking sides. He updated his September 3 post to say he had read my side, and his comments would stand.

Oh well, I thought at the time. The world is full of idiots.

By February 2013, my Parkinson's disease had advanced to the point where I had to use a cane for every day walking around. It was starting to affect my voice, but I was still capable of doing a live radio show on Blog Talk Radio.

My main focus at the time was pointing out the fraudulent activities of Ali A. Akbar – a convicted felon and head of the "National Bloggers Club, Inc." which had claimed a 501(c)3 status it did not have – Aaron Walker, the fired, disgraced lawyer who created the "Everybody Draw Mohammed Day" blog to inflame Islamic extremists but did so under a pseudonym, and then interjected himself under that pseudonym in a lawsuit between Kimberlin and some nobody little blogger. When Kimberlin learned Walker's true identity, Walker was fired by his employer – a home health care provider in Fairfax, Virginia, where he was a compliance attorney. Although Walker lies about the reason for his firing on his blog, the lawyer appointed to "take out the trash" noted Walker was fired for blogging on company time, letting company business go undone while he pursued Kimberlin, and for drawing unwanted attention to the home health care firm that really did not want to be known as the employer of a person who would intentionally inflame Islamic extremists.

I was also focused on Lee Stranahan, the former pornog apher, pimp, and conman who hopped from town to town with his family in tow, living in cars, motel rooms and eventually settling in Dallas after having a "Road to Damascus" moment when he met and was "saved" by the late conservative muckraker, Andrew Breitbart.

Walker and Stranahan were the subjects of most of the mockery and satire on the show. And shortly before going on the air on Valentine's Day 2013, I became aware that Stranny had filed charges against me. Two charges, actually. Harassment and Electronic Mail Harassment.

Let's examine the two laws under which I was charged.

Maryland Criminal Law Section 3-803 and 3-805.

§ 3-803. Harassment
(a) Prohibited. -- A person may not follow another in or

about a public place or maliciously engage in a course of conduct that alarms or seriously annoys the other:

(1) with the intent to harass, alarm, or annoy the other;

(2) after receiving a reasonable warning or request to stop by or on behalf of the other; and

(3) without a legal purpose.

(b) Exception. -- This section does not apply to a peaceable activity intended to express a political view or provide information to others.

(c) Penalty. -- A person who violates this section is guilty of a misdemeanor and on conviction is subject to:

(1) for a first offense, imprisonment not exceeding 90 days or a fine not exceeding $ 500 or both; and

(2) for a second or subsequent offense, imprisonment not exceeding 180 days or a fine not exceeding $ 1,000 or both.

And let us not forget…

§ 3-805. Misuse of electronic communication or interactive computer service.

(a) Definitions. --

(1) In this section the following words have the meanings indicated.

(2) "Electronic communication" means the transmission of information, data, or a communication by the use of a computer or any other electronic means that is sent to a person and that is received by the person.

(3) "Interactive computer service" means an information service, system, or access software provider that provides or enables computer access by multiple users to a computer server, including a system that

provides access to the Internet and cellular phones.
(b) Prohibited. --1) A person may not maliciously engage in a course of conduct, through the use of electronic communication, that alarms or seriously annoys another:
(i) with the intent to harass, alarm, or annoy the other;
(ii) after receiving a reasonable warning or request to stop by or on behalf of the other; and
(iii) without a legal purpose.
(2) A person may not use an interactive computer service to maliciously engage in a course of conduct that inflicts serious emotional distress on a minor or places a minor in reasonable fear of death or serious bodily injury with the intent:
(i) to kill, injure, harass, or cause serious emotional distress to the minor; or
(ii) to place the minor in reasonable fear of death or serious bodily injury.
(c) Construction of section. -- It is not a violation of this section for any of the following persons to provide information, facilities, or technical assistance to another who is authorized by federal or State law to intercept or provide electronic communication or to conduct surveillance of electronic communication, if a court order directs the person to provide the information, facilities, or technical assistance:
(1) a provider of electronic communication;
(2) an officer, employee, agent, landlord, or custodian of a provider of electronic communication; or
(3) a person specified in a court order directing the provision of information, facilities, or technical assistance to another who is authorized by federal or State law to intercept or provide electronic communication or to conduct surveillance of electronic

communication.

(d) Exception. -- Subsection (b)(1) of this section does not apply to a peaceable activity intended to express a political view or provide information to others.

(e) Penalty. -- A person who violates this section is guilty of a misdemeanor and on conviction is subject to imprisonment not exceeding 1 year or a fine not exceeding $ 500 or both.

Both of these laws require several things to be true before a person can be charged. The person must be told to cease contact. And I admit, Stranny told me to stop contacting him. I maintained that as a freelance reporter, it was my duty to contact him to ask questions before printing stories about him, in case he was interested in his side of the story being told.

Aaron Walker, after assisting Stranahan in the filing of his charge in the Howard County District Court, real zed he had to qualify for that "Stop Contacting Me" part of the law. So, on Feb. 14, he sent me this e-mail:

From: Aaron Worthing (edmd5.20.10@gmail.com);
Date: Thu, Feb 14, 2013 at 2:30 PM
Subject: CEASE AND DESIST
To: grouchcast@comcast.net, editor@liberalgrouch.com, bill@patriotombudsman. com
Dear Mr. Schmalfeldt,
As I am sure you are aware, there is a statute in Maryland prohibiting the use of electronic communications in order to harass another. Specifically I am referring to Md. Code Crim. Law §3-805 which states that:

(To which he successfuly copied and pasted the law to which he refers.)

As I am sure you can see, §3-805(b)(2) states that the law is not violated until the person asks you to stop. And then any further communication after that request And while again, I cannot give you legal advice, I can tell you how I interpret this law. I do not believe that any prosecution of yourself for harassment presents any First Amendment issues. We are not telling you that you cannot speak about us to third parties and to the world at large, we are only seeking to stop the conduct of directing communications to us and our associates. And indeed any prosecution would actually tend to vindicate free speech rights.

We both know you are doing this at the behest of Brett Kimberlin–or more precisely you are doing this at the behest of Neal Rauhauser, who made this request at the behest of Brett Kimberlin. And we know you are doing this solely to harass and intimidate us as a means of trying to bully us into silence about the very real wrongdoing Mr. Kimberlin is involved in. This harassment is not free speech, and it is designed to punish the free speech of others. And I will add that you are not serving in the slightest bit in a journalistic function. You are simply a thug–a paid one, if you have any intelligence–trying to suppress truth you don't want to be heard in public. You do not seek truth. You have never demonstrated the slightest bit of balance or fairness in this story, which is why, for instance, you never even acknowledged that Brett Kimberlin attempted to frame me for a crime, or even tried to explain, for instance, how his claim that I "decked" him could be reconciled with the security footage, to pick the most blatantly obvious example of Mr. Kimberlin's falsehoods under oath. Indeed when I pointed out the yawning mistakes in your writing, you never issued a correction or an update.

Still, this should not be taken as legal advice and I recommend that you consult with a lawyer (not Brett Kimberlin) to determine what the law is and what your duties are under it.

Sincerely,

Aaron "Worthing" Walker, Esq.

This one, I responded to.

Are you paid by the defeat? Because your track record of late would indicate you don't know what you're talking about.

Toodles. And write any time.

See you in court.

Bill

On the same day, Walker filed the same two charges as Stranny, with the addition of a request for a temporary peace order.

Now, Hoge wanted in on the fun. He felt no need to send dditional warnings for me to stop contacting him. He asserted on his complaint that he had demanded twice that I cease contact.

Here's the first such demand, from a blog post dated September 16, 2012… a couple weeks after he first mentioned me.

He wrote, "I don't feed trolls. I have received troll tweets and blog comments. If you're trolling, save your breath. I'll block your comments here and ignore you on Twitter."

The blog post was not directed to me.. It didn't mention me.

His "second warning" came later. Feb. 15, 2013. One day after Walker filed his charges Hoge posted on his blog that the September 16 "warning" was his first effort to get me to stop contacting him, since he clearly wrote "save your breath". In his Feb. 15 post, he was more direct, advising @oldunclebastard, @occupyrebellion and @breitbartunmasked to stop Tweeting him. At once.

Again, no mention of me by name. Just by Twitter address. He mentioned two other folks as well, but they were never charged.

On Feb. 18, Hoge charged me with the same two charges as Walker and Stranny. He added a charge of "Unauthorized Access to a Computer," making the following false allegation under penalty of perjury

This is a screencap from his charging document.

I know the blogger who run lonely conservative.com, Kara Beseth. She did not make the comment. It came from a static IP 50.115.175.148 that at the time belonged to Bill Schmalfeldt (aka, the Liberal Grouch, Patriot Ombudsman, Old Uncle Bastard). There is evidence, including Twitter messages ("tweets") sent by Schmalfeldt, that he is employed by Neal Rauhauser (aka Breitbart Unmasked, Occupy Unmasked, Cunto 2000, The Gaped Crusader). There is further evidence, including testimony under oath by Kimberlin, that Rauhauser is an employee of or business partner of Kimberlin (aka Occupy Rebellion).

Not me.

Please note that the IP Address was registered by a siteknown as www.holyis.com. The owner lives in Brazil. I am not about to share my IP address here. But it is not and has never been 50.115.175.148, and Mr. Hoge would have to have to prove that was in fact an IP address I OWNED and OPERATED on October 29, 2012.

He called his "discovery" further evidence that I "conspired with Brett Kimberlin and Neal Rauhauser" to "SWAT" him, and only called off the raid because law enforcement caught on..

My last tweet to Hoge before this was, I believe, on Feb. 19, 2013 for the LEGAL purpose of asking if he or his son (who sent me a photo of himself polishing a gun) were behind the spate of death threats I had been receiving. As there is currently no black letter law stating that a request to "cease contact" by a tweet or email carries any force of law, and there is no ruling on whether sending an "@mention" with someone's name when that person has asked you to cease contact carries any force of law. As I have suggested previously, Twitter is not a direct messaging application. It is a communications platform. If I send a message with the "@wjjhoge" moniker on it, it can be seen by Mr. Hoge, anyone following Mr. Hoge, and anyone following me. It is not of necessity meant ONLY for the eyes of Mr. Hoge, as a direct message would be. Since Mr. Hoge did not "follow" me on Twitter, nor did I him, sending a direct message to him is impossible.

As seen on Mr. Hoge's complaint, page six, he seemed to want to deny me the opportunity to earn any money with my writing and my communication with the outside world as he is insisting that all my electronic devices be "taken into evidence."

> **APPLICATION FOR STATEMENT OF CHARGES (CONTINUED)** Page 4 of 4
>
> have computers, smart phones, media storage devices (including, but not limited to, flashdrives, hot drives CDs, DVDs, and iPods), tablets (such as iPads), and remote servers in their possession or control that contain evidence relating to these crimes and that will be destroyed, hidden, or compromised unless taken into evidence.

Stranahan's charges were dismissed by the Howard County State's Attorney. So were Walker's. I still had permanent peace order, an event I wrote about on my Patriot-Ombudsman.com blog at the time, on March 22, 2013.

I sat in utter horror and delight as I watched a Howard County Judge rip every shred of flesh from Aaron Walker's body, leaving only a shambling, shaking skeleton.

How do I compare the feeling?

Ever been bothered by a yappy dog that kept you awake at night? You lay there, wishing someone would find a way to shut the damn dog up?

This was like watching as someone took the hated beast by the scruff and threw it into a woodchipper. Part of you is horrified by the sight. But another part of you is glad you'll get a good night's sleep for once.

Aaron Walker and John Hoge knew that Brett Kimberlin drove a gold Prius for the last court appearance. So they set Hoge's loathsome son, Little Hoggy, as a lookout in the parking lot, camera in hand. Waiting. We glided past without his notice in a black SUV BK rented for the day.

After getting some pics of Little Hoggy's futile searching, we made our way to the courthouse. Big Hoggy and Alfalfa Walker arrived, spoke to Little Hoggy for awhile, and made him wait out in the car. Then they came into the courthouse and looked surprised and terrified to see us there, waiting for them.

They took a seat on a bench. I maneuvered my roller walker to where I could sit and stare at them. One thing about Parkinson's disease. Sitting very still and not blinking comes natural. I drilled holes in Walker's head with my laser focus. Every now and again he would turn to see if I was still staring at him. I would smile and he would turn away quickly.

Eventually, my lawyer — the affable and well-liked in the Howard County Court House Tae H. Kim — arrived, we chatted, and went into Courtroom 5.

There were several cases to be heard ahead of ours. These were actual cases. Real people with real issues of real suffering, needing real protection. I personally gave my best wishes to a nice lady who was beaten to a fare-thee-well earlier in the day by her live-in companion, who was currently cooling his heels in the lockup. The judge granted her peace order and I told her I would pray for her safety.

Mr. Kim tapped me on the shoulder and said, "THIS is what this court is for. REAL cases involving real life and death danger. Not THIS bullshit." He gestured to Walker and Hoge who, if they have souls, HAVE to have been wondering how their penny ante bullshit case would be seen by the judge after a long afternoon of real tragedy.
When our case was called, Walker — as the complainant — gave his opening statement. Then it was Mr. Kim's turn. It was like watching, again in horror and disbelief, as Mike Tyson laid waste to a paraplegic. Walker was outclassed, outgunned, outprepared, and out-THOUGHT!

When Walker began to present his exhibits, mostly from Tweets from my timeline, he put me on the witness stand. He began by offering to do anything to help accommodate my Parkinson's disease, and both my lawyer and the judge told him to quit being cute and get to his case.

How do I put this? Walker. Aaron Walker. The man known to his readers as Aaron Worthing…

MADE MY CASE FOR ME!

He had me read many of my better tweets aloud. One, "@aaronworthing couldn't find the crack of his ass with a GPS device" had the judge turning his head and covering his mouth to stifle a laugh. It was clear that each Tweet I read meant doom for Walker's case. The judge decided early on that Twitter was a bulletin board where WHATEVER a person posts can be seen by anyone who looks for it.

Walker presented his e-mail to me in which he told me to never contact him again. I never received it, so he resent it along with another one in which he added four paragraphs of insults. Mr. Kim asked him which part of the insults were meant to ensure I would never contact him again. "It's like you said, 'You dirty bastard, you stink, you smell bad, you're stupid. Now, don't respond." The judge agreed.

"You can't let the snake out of the box and then tell people to stop hitting it," Judge Ricardo Daniel Zwaig told Walker.

After a torturous two hours, where Walker actually asked me to verify tweets sent to others by others, which the judge told him he couldn't do, hizzoner asked this grade school wannabe lawyer a simple question.

"You are a lawyer, Mr. Walker. Do you know what the word 'relevance' means?"

When Walker finished presenting his case, Mr. Kim didn't have to say a word. This was the easiest money Mr. Kim every made. The judge began to dress down Walker the way a stern but loving uncle dresses down a naughty nephew. He told him that he made MY case for me. That as a journalist with a blog, he can't tell a reader "never contact me" and then keep mentioning that reader. Mr. Kim, earlier, asked him why he listened to my radio show. Walker said he had to because he was gathering evidence. "Did someone force you to listen?" Mr Kim asked. "I had to so I could get evidence," Walker said again. "Did someone come down to Virginia, put a gun to your head, tell you to go to Mr. Schmalfeldt's Blog Talk Radio URL and FORCE you to listen?"

"No," Walker said sheepishly.

It was over. The judge told Walker that he can not claim to be a journalist, which he did in his opening statement, and then tell readers to not comment on what he's written. The judge reaffirmed what I've said all along, an "@mention" is not the same thing as forcing someone to read a letter, or answer a phone call, or a knock at the door. You can BLOCK a Twitter account. In fact, at one point when Walker asked me to verify something Patterico wrote to others, I said I hadn't seen the Tweet because I have Patterico blocked and therefore do not see what he writes.

Judge Zwaig explained the law to Walker. He told Walker he had not met the burden of proof required to get a peace order. He said the law offered no basis for relief. He sent Mr. Walker on his way.

The baliff asked if anyone wanted a copy of the dismissal.

"I do," I said.

"No thanks," Walker said. "I know what they look like."

"You've seen enough of them," I said as Mr. Kim laughed and slapped me on the shoulder.

Walker then began to whine about the presence of Brett Kimberlin in the courtroom and asked the Judge to make Kimberlin stay until he left because Brett Kimberlin was very scary. All 120 lbs., 5-nothing of him. The judge said Mr. Kimberlin was free to do whatever he likes. And Walker, with Hoge in tow, fled the courtroom with their tails between their legs like scalded pups.

Chapter 4 – SATISFIED? NOT HARDLY

One would be forgiven for thinking that getting his peace order would have satisfied Hoge.

One would be incorrect.

He claimed in an April 6, 2014 post that I had been harassing me for 2-1/2 years, which is a lie since I was only vaguely aware of him until he filed charges against me.

But someone was being harassed.

Can you guess who?

Blogs have "tags". When you write about something, you generally assign it a "tag" so if folks are interested in looking up what you've written about a certain subject, all they have to do is click the "tag" and every blog post you've written with that tag will show up.

So, how many blog posts Hoge write about me?

Using the #Cabin Boy Bill Schmalfeldt tag? – 505

Using the #Bill Schmalfeldt tag? – 39

With #BillSchmalfeldt in the title? – 110

With "Bill Schmalfeldt" in the post? – 482

He also claims I'm a stalker. But who is stalking who?

This is from a Sept. 26, 2013 post – the day I joined the

Society of Professional Journalists.

He accused me of "bragging" that I was a member of the SPJ, which he referred to as "our club."

He included a screencap, redacted, of his membership data.

General Information

Username:	wjjh ▆▆▆
Member ID:	▆▆▆
Join Date:	▆▆▆▆▆▆
Member Type:	Retired Member
Informal Name:	
Prefix:	▢
First Name:	WJJ
Middle Initial:	
Last Name:	Hoge
Suffix:	▢
Title:	Owner
Gender:	▢
Birth Date:	12/31/1947
Chapter:	
E-mail (only one address):	▆▆▆▆▆▆
Web Site (no e-mail addresses):	hogewash.com

So, why redact the membership data?

Here's why. Same post.

Yawn.

UPDATE—Apparently, the Cabin Boy has his panties in a knot because I'm a member of SPJ.

Bill Schmalfeldt @Fite_Rite_Radio   14m
I joined it. So no. I don't believe you when you say Hoge won't show his join date because it would prove he's a ▮▮▮▮ fraud. Sorry.
Collapse   ← Reply   ⟲ Retweet   ★ Favorite   ••• More

7:55 PM - 26 Sep 13 · Details

He objected to being called a (redacted) fraud. His breathless readers were treated to a retelling of the Hoge the Journalist story, he he began doing broadcast news while I was still in high school.

I think he said it best.

"Yawn."

THEN, THE ALLEGED EXTORTION

On Feb. 11, 2014 I was warned that it would be "unwise" for me to try his patience.

On Feb. 17, 2014, he repeated the threat, reminding me that although he wasn't interested in drawing me into the lawsuit Brett Kimberlin had filed against him and others, "not all the other defendants necessarily agree…"

On April 22, 2014, after strangling "My Slow, Journalistic Death" in its e-book crib, he gloated that he hoped he was "done" with me… for now… and that it would be "wise" for me to "give it a rest."

On April 23, 2014, he shared with his loving readers that everything I try ends up in my proving myself to be a "bigger fool, a sorrier sore loser." He doubted that I had "enough sense" to leave him alone. "I expect he will do something stupid," he wrote.

You read that correctly. The harasser is telling his readers that he doubts that the person he is harassing has enough sense to lay there and accept his harassment with good manners and a smile.

Unbelievable.

Chapter 5 – THE ANAL RAPE ENTHUSIAST

Hoge and his minions enjoy lying about my record as a writer, pretending the lie is the truth, then referring to the lie and citing it in other publications as being a true thing.

For instance, the "fact" that I was "fired" from the Daily Kos for writing an "anal rape fantasy."

Here is the article, posted May 18, 2012, still available at http://www.dailykos.com/story/2012/05/18/1092708/-The-REAL-Conservative-Case-Against-Gay-Marriage#:

My friends at Little Green Footballs step forward today with a compelling, scholarly article about why Conservatives fear gay marriage. If I may borrow a paragraph?

Could this be the correct explanation of the fear? Could it be that conservatives (subconsciously?) believe that if same-sex marriage were to become more accepted and hence more common, heterosexuals would actually begin converting their sexual orientation? Could conservatives really (subconsciously?) believe that gay sex is so much better than straight sex, or that switching one's sexual preference is, at least for most people, as easy as switching brands? It sounds silly, but you do often hear conservatives fantasizing about gay folks - especially teachers - "recruiting" children who would otherwise be straight, as if changing or determining someone's sexual orientation - even a child's - were as easy as giving them the right sales pitch!

As usual, the good folks at LGF are on to something. But I say the reasons why Conservatives -- especially MALE conservatives -- have such dread of gay marriage are much more simple and selfish.

It's the "Butt Stuff."

Male conservatives are convinced that gay men want to put their ying yangs in THEIR BUTTS! This is a horrifying prospect to your average, stupid male. This is why a blanket recognition that being gay is a normal variant of human sexuality, to these small, frightened, uneducated men, means society is saying it's OK for these gay men to put their willy-wallys in YOUR pooter hole!

Follow the logic.

Most stupid men, married or otherwise, enjoy pornography. They enjoy watching men with their throbbing, erect whatchamacallits do degrading thing to women with them. Slapping them on the face with it. Spanking them with it. There is no orifice on a woman's body that is safe from the probing, pulsating prongs on the popular pornos. And that includes the pooter hole. There's a whole SUBSET of pornography DEVOTED to anal sex. They give an AWARD at the ADULT VIDEO AWARDS each year to the actress involved in the most erotic Anal Sex scene.

So, it's not anal sex (as a practice) to which these small, frightened men object.

Heck, if you're a man and you're honest with yourself, you LIKE being on the *"doling it out"* end of anal sex. How many heterosexual men reading this diary right now have never asked their wife or girlfriend to just take a deep breath, relax, *"I'll just put in the tip and we'll see how it goes,"* and then you ram it home like Captain Kidd jamming his sword back into his scabbard while she hollers *"takeitouttakeitouttakeitout"* and you tell her to just relax and it won't hurt so bad and she starts kicking and screaming *"takeitOUTtakeitOUTtakeitOUT youfuckingbastardpieceofshit"* and you finally do *(because the walls are thin and your neighbors just LOVE calling the cops)* and you tell her she should have at least given herself a chance to relax and enjoy it and she (if she's your wife) doesn't let you anywhere near her with "that thing" for weeks and if she's your girlfriend she stops returning your calls?

So. We've established we have no problem with the theory of anal sex. Or the theory of oral sex, for that matter. If you're clean and perform proper hygienic maintenance "down there", most women will be more than happy from time to time to engage in this particular activity. And fellows, you know that this is a two way street, right? T'is well and good to give and receive.

So, no problem with oral sex.

Same sex? Shoot, that's fine too! As long as it's woman on woman.

This is as old as time itself. Why do you think the Bible not only authorizes but condones multiple wives for the biblical patriarchs? Because after a hard day of patriarching, there's nothing a patriarch likes better than to come home to watch some hot "wife on wife" action (they didn't *have* Blu-Ray or DVDs then) before jumping into the wife pile.

Now, with our modern technology, we love watching the ladies do other ladies. If you are married or in a relationship and your wife or girlfriend comes home with an attractive friend, and says *"Happy Birthday, honey"* as she and her friend peel off their clothes revealing their Victoria's Secret scanties as they hop onto the bed and start kissing and fooling around for awhile before beckoning you to join them, would you throw your hands up in Conservative horror and quote Leviti-cus? NO! You'd be on that bed, living the dream! Oh *HAPPY* day! What a *HAPPY* day!

So. Let's review. It's not anal sex as a practice that we find loathsome. Nor is it oral sex. Same sex is not a problem either, as long as those same sexes happen to be two or more women.

(Ever wonder why the Bible never condoned a woman having more than one husband? I think it was comedian Wanda Sykes who asked if anyone had ever come home from work to find his wife watching a man-on-man porno saying, "Yeah, baby. Ooooh. He likes that, doesn't he? Oh, yeah, baby. Give it to him!")

Therefore, if the Conservative male has no problem with anal sex, oral sex or same sex sex, why the problem with Gay Marriage?

It can't be the reason they constantly give,"because it threatens the sanctity of marriage."

I've been married three times. My wife #3 and I have been together since 1988. The first two failed because I was married to women who couldn't keep their pants on when I was not around. "Teh Gay" had nothing to do with it.

So, the real reason people are against Gay Marriage comes down to one of two things.

1. You are a closeted homosexual, self-loathing, raised in a household that forbade and punished "those kinds of thoughts". You have repressed these feelings, have gotten married and have children but can only find real sexual satisfaction with the kind of anonymous sex initiated with a game of "tappy toe" in a Minneapolis Airport Bathroom. Or,

2. You are ignorant heterosexual who -- because YOU would gladly fuck a warm piece of liver if no one was looking -- believes that all gay men will find YOU attractive and want to force their sexual attentions on YOU! Men over 40 don't even like going to the doctor because they know the doc will stick a well-lubricated, gloved finger "up there." The idea of being run to ground by hoards of pantless gay men with their throbbing manhoods acting like divining wands in the

search for "virgin ass" terrifies you. And you KNOW that's the next step. You KNOW that's what gays REALLY want... not monogamous relationships with people they love. Hell, YOU have a monogamous relationship with someone YOU love and yet every time you go out of town on a business trip you're balls deep in some hooker you met on Craigslist by 11:13 pm! That's why you're against gays in the military. All gays want to have sex with YOU! You just KNOW it. So if you were in the Army and had to take a shower with GAY people looking at you, it would be a constant battle to maintain your anal virginity. If you were in a FOXHOLE (God forbid) with a GAY, then nobody would be securing the perimeter because you would be too busy securing your ANUS against this GAY guy who you just KNOW wants to fuck you. Oh sure, he's sitting over there nice and quiet and writing a letter to his sister. But YOU know what he's thinking. HE'S thinking about waiting until you're asleep, sliding down your fatigues and DOING THINGS to you!

THAT is the problem with gay marriage. It's not the fact that it's same sex have sex with the same sex (as long as it's only women). It's not that anal sex is disgusting, because who hasn't tried to get away with it at least once in a heterosexual relationship (sorry, honey... I missed!) or that we find oral sex to be immoral and de facto sodomy (which we don't even when we say we do).

The bottom line (*giggle*) is that stupid straight people are scared that rampaging hoards of GAYS are going to

ATTACK THEM and FORCE THEIR wing wangs up their pooter holes and OBAMA SAYS IT'S OK NOW!

THAT'S **the problem!**

So, were you horrified? Neither was I. Granted, my taste for satire isn't the same as everyone else. But this column so offended a small group of professional victims that they "hide rated" the diary into oblivion and I was banned from DK for objecting.

This, gentle reader, was grist for the Hoge mill, and that mill always needs gristing!

Chapter 6 – IT'S NOT JUST HOGE

There is a cancer in the former Andrew Breitbart body politic. How deep does it go? Has it gotten into the system where it can spread to the rest of the body? Or is it something that can be cut out, studied, learned from, and then saved in a laboratory of investigative journalism? When Breitbart died on March 1, 2012, did the cancer die with him? Or was his death the thing that caused the cancer to spread? Every metastatic cancer has what's called a "sentinel node". That's the lymph node that indicates to the trained observer that the cancer has spread and something must be done if the patient is to be saved.But is this patient one who CAN be saved? How widespread is the disease? Is it too late?

This cancer keeps popping up in one organ after another.

Now, it seems to have reached the office of the Los Angeles County District Attorney.

Let's examine the other organs to which this cancer has already been identified. After all, Breitbart had a wide circle of friends who also blogged in the conservative ether.

Aaron Walker and his pathological obsession with a crime committed some 40 years ago, where the criminal has served his time, paid his debt, and now wishes to live a quiet life as a liberal activist. Walker lost his job as a lawyer after he was the driving force behind the "Everyone Draw Mohammed Day" that caused widespread violence, death and destruction in the Middle East.

Robert Stacy McCain, who sobers up long enough to write anti-semitic, racist diatribes that allegedly got him kicked out of a Seventh Day Adventist compound he once inhabited.

Ali Abdul Razaq Akbar, a two-bit gay ghetto thug from Fort Worth who went from the jail cell to the heights of the Young Republican establishment, showing that the old maxim "It's not Who You Know, It's Who You Blow" rings true. (Cough – Karl Rove. Cough. Cough.)

Mandy Nagy, the otherwise inoffensive but deluded right wing hack who wrote for Breitbart's various websites, who now finds herself leaderless, rudderless, and everybody's victim.

The rot-toothed turncoat **Lee Stranahan**, who was a liberal pornographer (some of his photos are currently being investigated to see if the models were legally old enough to have naked bondage pictures taken of them), who had a "Paul on the Road to Damascus" conversion after meeting Breitbart and is now one of the most obsequious, obnoxious, self-important publicity-seeking turds in the overflowing, filthy toilet of the Breitbart Memorial Empire.

And leave us not forget **Patrick Frey.**

Patrick Frey.

Patterico.

When I was a federal employee (until March 2011 when my Parkinson's disease caused me to retire), I had to live under the constraints of the Hatch Act. At work, I was not allowed to write or say anything that promoted a partisan candidate, a political party, etc.

In my private writing, I had to make sure there was no connection between my official duties and my private thoughts.

How is it that a Deputy District Attorney in Los Angeles County is allowed to keep his job, living off the proceeds of county, state and federal taxes collected from the people of the county, the state of California and the taxpayers of the United States of America, when it turns out he was not only directly involved in what appears to be the commission of a crime, close association with a known criminal, and attempts to harass a person who claims sexual harassment at the hands of the above mentioned "known criminal"?

Deputy District Attorney, Patrick Frey, is also a well-known conservative blogger known as "Patterico." He blogs under the title "Patterico Pontificates." We have had our own mixups with Frey in the past, but those are not at issue now.

What is at issue, is this legal filing that alleges Mr. Frey and his wife, also of the District Attorney's office — both public servants — both officers of the court — two people who took an oath to "serve, protect and defend the Constitution of America"– were not only friends with convicted Breitbart hoaxter James O'Keefe (he of the pimp costume, the fraudulent ACORN video, the attempt to smear Shirley Sherrod at the USDA, and the event that finally crossed the line — the attempt to tap into the telephone lines of California Congresswoman Maxine Waters), but may have KNOWN that O'Keefe intended to break the law with his attempted wiretap of Rep. Water's office in advance and failed to report it, as required by a duly sworn officer of the court.

That's what's alleged in this court document, filed Oct. 2.

You can read the entire filing for yourself here. It's a sordid affair, if true, of county officials using the power of their offices to advance a partisan political agenda. The filing alleges that Mr. Frey used his office to harass a private citizen who may have been involved in a criminal conspiracy with O'Keefe, who O'Keefe allegedly drugged and tried to take sexual advantage of, and, in his "Patterico Pontificates" blog, wrote alleged defamatory and untrue things about the woman who attempted to come forward to explain her connection with O'Keefe.

Again, read the entire filing. Then, ask yourself.

Would any of this nonsense be going on if Andrew Breitbart hadn't died? If "Daddy" was still running things in the Breitbart empire, would Lee Stranahan be under investigation for possible child pornography and pimping out his own wife? Would Ali Akbar be sending out chuckling little tweets, reeking of his own hubris, about how he is untouchable by law? Would the National Bloggers' Club have done things legally if Breitbart had lived, or would they have pretended to be a legitimate 501(c)3, which they are not?

And while we're at it.

If Breitbart were still alive, would he have pulled back the reins on people like the besotted R. Stacy McCain

("The OTHER McCain")? Would he have, by now, told Aaron Walker (Worthing?) to shut his cake hole and get a job? Would Michelle Malkin have sought the services of the American Center for Law and Justice to "defend" Ali Akbar and the National Bloggers Club, or would he have known that there was at least one alleged rotten apple in the ACLJ barrel in the form of former ACLJ senior counsel and Regent University Adjunct Law Professor James M. Henderson, Sr., who was either forced to resign, was fired, or for whatever reason has been erased from all memory on the ACLJ website since this blog and Exposed Politics made public the allegations that the married father of eight was involved in exchanging money, alcohol and drugs in exchange for being on the receiving end of anal sex with a variety of young men over the last few years, at least one of which we have established was not quite 18 when Henderson, under an assumed name (that didn't fool his victims — if his over-18 year old paramours can be called victims — legally, in Virginia, the age of consent is 18)?

Would Breitbart, who was addled but not crazy and certainly not stupid, have made sure he surrounded himself with people who were trustworthy? Or does his drunken rant videotaped shortly before his death, screaming "STOP RAPING PEOPLE", only apply to liberals?

I'm no doctor, although I did play one on the radio.

This cancer has spread to far too many organs for this patient to survive. You can smell the rot, seeping through the pores. Each breath has the sickeningly

sweet stench of decay. The body is a shell, more tumor than useful tissue at this point.

It's time for the authorities, whoever monitors the legal (and illegal) activities of people who write lies on the Internet, who deal in prostitution and child pornography, who defraud people of their hard earned cash because they don't believe in government welfare, but they're too lazy to actually work for a living, the people who lie for living in print, online, on the Internet and on Television, and the people who hide in the dark corners of the Net to prey on the young and stupid with promises of money, pot and booze as long as they'll take their pants off and play "pokey poopie" with you...

It's time for SOMEBODY to realize the cancer has spread too far to be cured.

It's time to pull the plug.

Perhaps one of the stinkiest turds in the bowl, right behind Hoge, is the execrable disgraced, fired, unemployed, unemployable lawyer, Aaron Walker.

This next segment is adapted from a series of posts on my Patriot-Ombudsman blog, written Oct. 29, 2012.

Every post on his blog, Allergic to Bull, contains the same pitch for cash towards the end.

My wife and I have lost our jobs due to the harassment of convicted terrorist Brett Kimberlin, including an attempt to get us killed and to frame me for a crime carrying a sentence of up to ten years. I know that claim sounds fantastic, but if you read starting here, you will see absolute proof of these claims using documentary and video evidence. If you would like to help in the fight to hold Mr. Kimberlin accountable, please hit the Blogger's Defense Team button on the right. And thank you…

Poor guy! Being harassed by a convicted terrorist and all. That claim sure does sound fantastic. Where do I dontate?

But wait a minute. What were the *actual* circumstances of Aaron Walker's dismissal?

After sifting through a large volume of documents received from a source wishing to remain anonymous, we have determined — from Walker's own e-mails at the time and correspondence from his former employer that Walker was not fired because of any harassment, an attempt to get him killed, or because of being framed for a crime. Aaron Walker was fired because the law firm he worked for and its clients did not want to be the target of reprisals by potential Islamic extremists when Walker was identified as being behind an ill-advised effort to inflame the Islamic religious community with a little project called "Everybody Draw Mohammed Day."

Walker served as a counsel with the law firm of Hodges and Associates of Fairfax, VA. His primary client seemed to be Professional Healthcare Resources, Inc. (PHRI) in Annandale. Walker's office was at the same address as PHRI.

In addition to and, according to his former employer, sometimes instead of, providing legal service to PHRI,

Walker seemed to be obsessed with the subject of Islamic extremism and assisting a small time blogger named Seth Allen in his legal battle against Brett Kimberlin.

If taken at face value, the paragraph speaks of dire circumstances for Aaron Walker and his family.

My wife and I have lost our jobs due to the harassment of convicted terrorist Brett Kimberlin, including an attempt to get us killed and to frame me for a crime carrying a sentence of up to ten years. I know that claim sounds fantastic, but if you read starting here, you will see absolute proof of these claims using documentary and video evidence. If you would like to help in the fight to hold Mr. Kimberlin accountable, please hit the Blogger's Defense Team button on the right. And thank you.

The problem is? It just isn't true.

Aaron Walker, who blogs under the pseudonym Aaron Worthing, knew his real name was about about to be exposed thanks to the investigation of Brett Kimberlin, a person Walker and several of his confederates had been stalking, suing and otherwise harassing for no other reason than he is a liberal who was convicted of a crime nearly 40 years ago. Having served his time, Kimberlin is back in the community doing work for a progressive organization, and this drives Walker and his right wing allies nuts. We'll delve deeper into the war between Walker and Kimberlin, its origins and where things stand now in a later segment.

But for now, let's discuss the real reasons for the termination of Aaron Walker.

Walker was one of the driving forces behind a blog effort to inflame the passions of Islamic extremists around the world. This was already an open wound in the Islamic world — when a Danish cartoonist drew a cartoon of the prophet Mohammed. Islam has strict prohibitions of images depicting the prophet. In the Middle East, where passions run high, the streets were on fire because of this blasphemy in the eye of the Islamic world. By being a driving force supporting and celebrating a national Islamophobic orgasm of stupidity known as "Everyone Draw Mohammed Day" in 2010, what Walker seemingly wanted to do was open a fresh box of salt and pour it right on the open wound here in the American Islamic community in the hopes that they would also erupt in violence, giving American authorities even more reason to clamp down on them.

Yet, like most cowards, Walker wanted to provoke from a hidden position. He blogged under the name Aaron Worthing because he knew the negative attention that would come to the law firm he worked for and the health care organization for which he provided legal counsel would be adversely affected by the blowback.

We're talking about the sort of blowback which could come from a post like this one Walker made on his blog, everyonedrawmohammed.blogspot.com.

The blog is an "invited guest" blog now, so you have to ask Walker for permission to join so you can hate Muslims with him. Walker argued that it was his First Amendment right to write whatever he wanted to write, to draw whatever he wanted to draw, and he is absolutely correct. Even if you are inciting people to attract a violent response. Notice here how Walker would not accept a drawing under two circumstances — no porn, and the drawing must be outrageous and blasphemous enough to a Muslim as to invoke a fatwa.

And oh, how very brave, to throw down the gauntlet to the scary, scary Muslims... with a false name.

All perfectly legal. Cowardly, craven, simpering, but legal under the first amendment.

Yet, conservatives seem to have a basic misunderstanding of what the First Amendment does and does not do. The First Amendment says the government can pass no laws restricting your right to express your opinion. The First Amendment does *not* protect you from the reactions of other people expressing their First Amendment right to call you a bigot, a racist, an islamaphobe, and an idiot. The First Amendment does *not* guarantee that you have a right to anonymity. If someone wants to invest the time, effort and money to learn your real identity, that is within their right. And it is within their First Amendment rights to publicize your actual name and tie what you've written and said around your neck.

Brett Kimberlin, through sources, ascertained that Aaron Worthing was a Virginia lawyer named Aaron Walker. He was set to release this information in January 2012. Walker felt compelled to write a letter to his boss and coworkers.

This letter is part of a treasure trove of documents given to the Patriot-Ombudsman by a source requesting anonymity. We can affirm, however, that the party providing the information is not a named party in the ongoing civil case between Walker and Kimberlin.

We have reached out to Walker and his attorney, Dan Backer of DB Capitol Strategies PLLC for comment. Other than a "never write to me again" e-mail from Walker and veiled and silly threats about being dragged into court to answer subpoeneas for printing this publicly available information from Backer, there has been no comment from the Walker camp.

Even in his letter, Walker refuses to accept any responsibility for bringing this unwanted attention to himself and to his coworkers because of his blogging under a pseudonym.

It's everybody's fault but Aaron. It's Brett Kimberlin's fault for wanting to know his real name. It's the other redacted names' fault for working to learn the real name of someone bent on causing the American Islamic community to explode in anger. It's Seth Allen's fault for asking Walker for help. It's even Anthony Weiner's fault — somehow.

How did this letter go over with his employer? Let's just say... not well. But even in e-mails to friends and supporters, Walker just can not make himself accept any responsibility for his actions!

PHRI hired Walker to be a compliance counsel, not to be a muckraking blogger, inviting Islamic extremists to burn down the city. So, PHRI brought in a new legal gun, James Hodges of the firm Hodges and Associates of Fairfax, VA, to inform Mr. Walker that his services were no longer required or desired by PHRI.

About a month later, it seemed Mr. Hodges' fears of retribution had come true since Walker had *not* made it clear he was no longer working for PHRI.

As we've seen and as we shall see in future stories on this subject, it's all about Aaron Walker and everyone else can go to hell. It certainly did not take him long to reach out and put the finger on his friends and associates.

Again, what happened was everyone's fault BUT Aaron's.

Well, it's not ONLY Aaron's fault. He did work with others to get himself into this predicament. They hate Muslims,, too! AND Brett Kimberlin.

In our next installment we'll present what could pass as an Agatha Christie novel. But instead of the analytical acumen of Hercule Poirot, what we see is a gaggle of seemingly demented Miss Marple's darting about, working at cross purposes, stumbling, bungling, misreading clues, coming to incorrect conclusions, all the while worried that a Peeping Tom may be trying to peek into their windows to see them in their petticoats.

Seth Allen is a blogger. A legend in his own mind. He loves himself more than any mother ever loved a child. He blogs at a place called http://davefromqueens2.blogspot.com.

But he wanted more. He wanted to blog for Brad Friedman. But Brad said no. Brad did not recognize Seth's greatness.
    So Brad had to pay!

The "Just Call Me Lefty Blog" tells the tale.

...when he was not hired by Brad Blog he set about going after Brad Friedman and his business partner Brett Kimberlin with a vengeance which has continued to this day.

But what can you say about Brad Friedman? Oh, Seth TRIED. Various posts about unnamed sources advising him that Brad was a drug user and blah blah blah. But that was no way to really get back at Brad, not when he had a target-rich environment in Brad's partner, Brett Kimberlin.

And oh, my, how Seth vented his anger and need for revenge on Kimberlin. Eventually, Kimberlin sued Seth Allen for harassment and stalking. Allen was served with one subpoena after another, which he refused to accept. He reached out to someone he thought he could trust, a Virginia lawyer he knew as Aaron Worthing. In an e-mail to the Patriot-Ombudsman on Oct. 29, Seth explained how "Worthing" became involved in the Kimberlin case.

I did wonder if Aaron could defend me. But it turned out he is not allowed to practise law in Maryland. He scammed his way into my case, while Kimberlin was also wrong to prolong it. This isn't rocket science, and I'm under no obligation to spend any more time on this, especially with someone like yourself who has previously smeared me.

While we don't recall specifically smearing Mr. Allen — in fact, we recall it quite the other way around — we gave him a chance to respond to questions. He chose to be cute.

I am not going to reinvent the wheel and personally explain to you what I've already written. I started putting everything together once the big story hit on Patterico's smearing BK, Neal, and Ron ala SWATgate. Ali, Stranahan, and Darby then smeared me. I got no support from the NBC and obviously none from that superpac bitch Dan Backer.

Patterico is Los Angeles Deputy District Attorney Patrick Frey who blogs at "Patterico Pontificates." More on him later. Neal is Neal Rauhauser, someone thought by the Kimberlin-haters to be his right hand man. Ron is Ron Bryneart, with whom the Patriot-Ombudsman has had several run-ins of an unfriendly nature. Both Neal and Ron are named as co-defendants with Kimberlin in Aaron Walker's most recent suit. Ali is Ali Akbar, whom we have written about extensively. Same with Lee Stranahan. Brandon Darby is Stranahan's friend and partner. NBC is the ill-begotten National Bloggers Club, formed by Ali Akbar, originally referred to as a 501(c)3 organization, later debunked. SWATgate refers to the recent pattern of people having the police sent to their house by an anonymous caller pretending to be someone who has murdered his wife. Such fun games these children play.

A person with intimate knowledge of the case who requests anonymity claimed that Walker's involvement with Seth consisted of advising Seth on how to post articles about Kimberlin in such a way as to avoid a lawsuit. (We see how well that worked.) But it became clear to the Kimberlin side that Seth was getting outside legal help.

But Seth was out to get Kimberlin to punish Brad Friedman for not recognizing his genius.

After ignoring a number of served subpoenas, Allen showed up at a damages hearing after having a default judgement entered for his activities related to his harassment of Kimberlin. (Walker later came on board and tried to have the case overturned, but — according to someone with intimate knowledge of the case — by that time it was long past the stage where one could go in and ask for appeals or any other motions to be filed in the case.) After trying to argue law with the judge, Hizzoner asked a deputy in the courtroom why he was there. The answer? To arrest Seth Allen. Hilarity ensued.

Since that time, Seth has been more or less shuffled off to the side of this drama as an irrelevant figure, a footnote in the entertaining subtext of a very serious court case where a Judge will decide whether a person has a First Amendment right to reveal the name of a person who wishes to remain anonymous.

Not to say that Walker hasn't been in touch with Seth — under the table.

This part of the Aaron Walker saga will likely either remind you of a door-slamming British bedroom farce, or an Agatha Christie novel. And not with the analytical acumen of Hercule Poirot. More likely a gaggle of senile Miss Marple's, bumbling, stumbling, misinterpreting, working at cross-purposes while worrying that SOMEBODY has been trying to peek into their windows at night to see them in their petticoats.

We've already said much about Aaron Walker, who blogged as Aaron Worthing until his real identity was outed. (He is currently suing Brett Kimberlin, Ron Brynaert and Neal Rauhauser for revealing his true identity, which — to the best of my knowledge — is not against any law. It's a risk anyone takes by publishing under a pseudonym. I don't recall Samuel Clemens suing anyone for revealing he was Mark Twain. And did Joe Klein sue anyone when he was revealed as the "Anonymous" who wrote "Primary Colors?")

We've already met and disposed of Seth Allen.

Let's meet some of the other players in our little drama.

MANDY NAGY — Code Name: *"Liberty Chick"*. Former close associate of dead Andrew Breitbart. Writer at Breitbart.com. Writer of several stories to remind America that Brett Kimberlin was convicted of a crime some 40 years ago, a fact that needs to be hammered into the public consciousness over and over again because he's a liberal activist now. She worked for Breitbart, but she didn't seem to have a lot of faith in his ability to keep a secret.

PATRICK FREY — Code Name: *"Patterico"*. Deputy District Attorney for the County of Los Angeles, which is something like 3,000 miles away from Maryland and Virginia, where the legal action between Aaron Walker and Brett Kimberlin is being played out. Way out of his jurisdiction. We wonder how much of his time which should be spent doing the work for the people of the County of Los Angeles, California, is spent poking his nose into the Kimberlin case.

…because the fact that you are trying to destroy a person's reputation through legal harassment is best served when you remind the court of a crime committed some 40 years ago.

These are your three main players. These e-mail screen caps and other documents we've used in this series are part of a treasure trove of documents received by the Patriot-Ombudsman connected with the Walker/Kimberlin various legal actions. The person providing the documents has requested anonymity, although we are assured the person is not one of the parties in the legal actions.

The e-mail exchanges between Walker and Nagy and Frey mostly deal with plotting and planning strategy as well as proofing the learning-disabled Walker's briefs. (He has blogged about his learning disabilities, although we're not sure he refers to dyslexia or something else.)

In December of 2011, Walker laid out his reasons for believing he has a constitutional right to not have his name revealed as the author of the "Everybody Draw Mohammed Day" blog.

Meanwhile, the Deputy District Attorney of Los Angeles County wonders whether or not a sting operation might be the thing to link Neal Rauhauser to Brett Kimberlin.

Sneaky! For her part, Liberty Chick — impartial journo that she is — realizes they will need a non-Breitbart outlet for the story if they want anyone to give it credibility.

There were intensive e-mail exchanges between the three over the Christmas holiday in 2011 as they put their heads together to learn who, yes WHO, was peeping into the window to determine Walker's true identity.

Then, on January 7, 2012, the horrible news that everyone dreaded all along! After spending months trying to determine whether or not Neal Rauhauser and Brett Kimberlin exchanged Christmas Cards or met in passing in a mall parking lot… the horror! Walker's true identity was revealed.

When Walker knew the jig was up, that's when he wrote the letter to the HR staff at his employer, Professional Healthcare Resources, Inc. of Annandale, VA. After they read the letter, they hired Jim Hodges of Hodges and Associates, Fairfax, VA, to deliver the news to Walker that he was no longer an employee of PHRI, and to fumigate his office of the stench of Islamophobic hatred.

Of course, this was all Kimberlin's fault, Walker maintained.

As you have no doubt read in his "Allergic to Bull" blog:

My wife and I have lost our jobs due to the harassment of convicted terrorist Brett Kimberlin, including an attempt to get us killed and to frame me for a crime carrying a sentence of up to ten years. I know that claim sounds fantastic, but if you read starting here, you will see absolute proof of these claims using documentary and video evidence. If you would like to help in the fight to hold Mr. Kimberlin accountable, please hit the Blogger's Defense Team button on the right. And thank you.

Well, we've disposed of the phony reason for Walker being fired. It had nothing to do with Kimberlin and everything to do with PHRI wanting nothing to do with Walker's rabid Islamophobia. As far as the "attempt to get us killed," Walker maintains in his suit THAT was the ultimate end of Kimberlin's "outing" of Walker. The "framing" is a bit more complicated. According to someone with intimate knowledge of the case, Walker showed up in court on January 9, 2012 to a hearing in which Kimberlin was dealing with his defamation case against Seth Allen. You will recall that Walker was giving Allen some under-the-table legal advice. The source tells the Patriot-Ombudsman that Walker showed up unannounced and interrupted the Judge in the case several times to get him to redact and or seal his name on Kimberlin's motion to withdraw Walker as a witness in the Allen case.

The source says the Judge gave Walker what he wanted and sealed his name, then Walker and Kimberlin exited the courtroom together. Shortly, the source says, a scuffle ensued whereby Walker forcibly removed Kimberlin's iPad from him because Walker thought Kimberlin was trying to take his picture. Walker later told a different judge, the source said, that he thought Kimberlin had a bomb hidden in his iPad and was preparing to detonate it.

The source said, Walker (being a hero and all that) advanced on Kimberlin, a scuffle ensued, and Walker ripped the iPad away from Kimberlin.

Kimberlin sustained an injury to his one of his eyes, went to a doctor who then sent him to the hospital for a CT scan.

Walker claimed that Kimberlin lied about the alleged assault and forged documents claiming he went to the doctor. The assault was never charged or prosecuted.

The court battle between Kimberlin and Walker is set for a December 4th hearing. We are hard pressed to come up with a reason for a judge to grant that Walker has a constitutional right to remain anonymous while utilizing his First Amendment rights to inflame the passions of angry Muslims.

But, Walker is a lawyer. He is a right winger. The reasoning used by such people is not always linear in nature.

I am a liberal. But when it comes to writing a news story, even news commentary, I do try to be fair. That means, I try to give folks that I am going to write about a chance to tell their own side of the story. I wrote to Patrick Frey, but "Patterico" hasn't graced me with a response. I wrote to Mandy Nagy, but "Liberty Chick" is in New Jersey and may be dealing with storm issues. I wrote to Seth Allen, he replied and I used his replies in the story about him. I wrote to Aaron Walker.

He told me to never write to him again. He told me I should write to his lawyer, Dan Backer of DB Capitol Strategies. That is the firm associated with The Bloggers Defense Team which is another in a long line of money making schemes that Mr. Backer has been associated with. Take a look at the recent FilmLadd article that Todd Cefaratti has now joined the battle against Brett Kimberlin which The Bloggers Defense Team has been carrying on in the name of right wing Islamophobe attorney and blogger Aaron Walker aka Aaron Worthing.

Well? I wrote a letter to Backer. He responded.

Mr. Schmalfeldt,

Thank you for your email.

Pursuant to the Court's order in this matter, we will not comment in any way upon any documents that may or may not be discovery materials. We will not violate the judge's order with respect to Discovery and that includes neither acknowledging nor denying whether something is or is not part of the discovery that is under seal which would operate as a breach of the court's order.

You may "report" that any way you choose as is your right.

You would also be wise to confer with an attorney prior to your publication of any material that may be under a court-ordered seal to see whether you may be subject to a court order to disclose the sources of this information if it is in fact under such Court order. Whether or not press shield laws apply to you in particular and in this circumstance, they are not as absolute as you may presume, and I would strongly encourage you to be certain as to the scope of your potential liability before disclosing such information so you can make an informed decision.

Please do not contact my client again. You may direct inquiries to me.

Regards,

Dan Backer, Esq.

Right away with the, *"Booooooo, I'm a scary lawyer who KNOWS things, boooooooooo"* nonsense. I responded.

Thank you for your response. In the absence of an authoritative description of what documents are under seal, in the absence of a competent authority to tell me that THESE documents are under court seal, and since you have seen the document I sent to Mr. Walker and would — presumably — KNOW whether or not that is the kind of document covered by the court seal, I will feel confident... in the absence of countervailing opinion, that the documents I have are not under seal. I am endeavoring to determine which documents are actually under court seal. If it is your choice to be unhelpful in that regard, I understand completely, although I would argue you are not serving your client's interest by allowing publication of documents that you know to be under seal. If somewhere along the line a competent authority informs me that these documents are covered by the court seal, of course I will obey. But I am not going to withhold publication in the public interest because they MIGHT be under a court seal. I need to know if they ARE. Since I did not obtain them by illegal means, if they are under seal, I exhaust my responsibility to determine that fact by asking the attorneys involved. I have asked for a copy of the order, so we'll see what we have.

I'm sure you can see where I'm coming from.

Be well.

Bill Schmalfeldt.

He wasn't done trying to frighten me yet.

Mr. Schmalfeldt,

You can believe whatever you wish, but the facts are the facts. If you publish this information, you and you alone are responsible for the consequences. I have no duty to save you from violating a court's order or otherwise participating in conduct that creates liability for you.

I think you should seriously ask yourself if any reasonable person – let alone a journalist – in your situation would look at this bounty of information (which contains redacted personal information), and the source you got it from, and not think that it is either (a) subject to a court ordered seal or (b) the product of illegal access to someone's computer, or (c) the product of some other nefarious and/or unlawful activity. I find it rather dubious that you can in good conscience say that this information came to you in an honest manner and with clean hands. If you then republish that information, that's entirely your responsibility for doing so, and again I encourage you to seek counsel as to your liability in doing so before you do so.

You need not respond nor communicate with me any further on this. You're going to do what you're going to do and you're going to have to deal with the repercussions on you and your sources for doing so.

Regards,

Dan Backer, Esq.

Now, at this point, I am reminded of President Obama during his second debate with Gov. Romney. Obama knew right where Romney was about to step with his declaration that it took 14 days for Obama to mention "terror" in connection with the Benghazi attack. Romney was blundering toward a tiger trap and Obama was going to allow him to do so unabated.

"Proceed, Governor."

If I were about to write something that Backer really believed would help his client if it got published, wouldn't he have said, "Proceed, sir"? So, I responded.

Already checked, counselor. These documents not covered. Now, does your client wish to comment, or do I just go with his non-denial denial?

Mr. Schmalfedlt,

Again, I am asking you to cease any and all contact with my client. If you have any additional questions you may direct them to me alone.

I am not your lawyer and I am not going to give you legal advice, nor discuss with you the scope of what you think my legal responsibilities are. I have given you the courtesy of encouraging you to seek your own legal counsel before you do something that may (despite your belief in the matter) encumber upon you legal liabilities. You are entirely within your rights to choose not to do so.

I have given you the answer we are going to give you. Since I do not know what information you have in your possession nor where you came by such information, I obviously cannot comment on its origin, veracity, or whether it is under court ordered seal. Even if I could, doing so does not further the intent of the court with respect to its order or the legal interests of my client. Perhaps you should ask yourself if this information is the sort of thing that could possibly have come to you other than through the violation of the court ordered seal?

Thank you for your email and, in advance, for respecting my express request that you cease any and all communication with my client.

Regards,

Dan Backer, Esq.

Now it was time to let Mr. Backer know what I thought of him and his bloviating.

Dan. May I call you Dan?

I told you. Lawyers don't scare me. Let's examine your latest. It reeks of desperation. I did not respond with the proper amount of trembling to your last e-mail. You sat and thought about it for awhile and thought, "Damn, he's gonna write something."

I look through your message, scanning carefully for any sign that the aforementioned documents are under court ordered seal. I have reviewed the papers filed by both sides in this case, and I can find nothing, nada, zip, zilch stating that these particular documents fall under the Judge's seal order. You are employing your client's technique of creating a straw man. Not only did I NOT say that I plan to ignore the duty to reasonably inquire, I told you that I HAD inquired, contacting YOU was PART of that inquiry, and that I would review the filings in the case, and I am telling you now, I HAVE FOUND NOTHING SEALING THESE PARTICULAR DOCUMENTS!!!

Now, I know Aaron likes suing people. Since his company fired him, it's his primary source of income. Other than the illegal National Broadcaster's Club, that is, and his donation button on his blog. You want to file subpoenas? What are you going to subpoena? Which of these 300+ pages of e-mails and messages from Walker's former employer fall under the order?

You're going to drag me into court and force me, on the record, with my dulcet Broadcaster's Voice, to read each and every page of this information into the record? How is THAT serving your client?

You say "obviously" a lot. I am not obliged to reveal the source of my information, and like many of my predecessors in this field, I will park my nearly 58-year old Parkinson's disease stricken ass in jail rather than deliver that information. They still feed you in jail, right? And they'd have to put me in the hospital ward as I am unable to walk without assistance. Think of the money I'll save on pharmaceuticals as the county will be responsible for my medications — and they're expensive. I'm sure that, once I'm released, the court will want one of the parties to recompense the state for this expense. And I know people who would spend every minute of every day writing about how Dan Backer, Esquire, locked up a retired professional, now-turned freelance journalist, crippled with Parkinson's disease, on a hopped up charge. I will be on the phone with all major networks, where I have contacts and friends, and this will make for a DELIGHTFUL public interest story about how Dan Backer, in his vigorous defense of Aaron Walker, the cowardly little man who sued someone for revealing his last name, threw a public-minded, disabled Vietnam-era veteran with a crippling neurological disorder in jail because he refused to identify the source of some e-mails that make his client look foolish.

Aaron still has the chance to speak for himself. I would welcome the opportunity to interview him. But Dan? Bluster and bloviating just don't move me. It sure doesn't scare me.

If you know for a fact that these papers are covered by the court order, I adjure you as an officer of the court to divulge that information. If not, either make Walker available for an interview…. or dry up and blow away.

As Bill Murray said in the movie, "Scrooged" when the Ghost of Christmas Future crowded him in the elevator, "That kinda shit might work on the chicks, mister. But not with me."

Well. It *was* OK that I call him "Dan".

If you'd like.

Your assumptions are incorrect. You made it clear you would write something and that you intended to use this material, and from the outset I had no illusions as to

anything I might say would dissuade you from that course. I fully expect you to write about that content despite it being protected by a court order. But I've met my obligations to forewarn you.

Your analysis is incorrect. The judges' October 5th Order, which is publically available, clearly states that all Discovery responses are to be filed under seal and for the parties eyes only. We filed all our discovery under seal pursuant to the judges' orders. I clearly stated in my last email that this information was part of our discovery and thus subject to the judges' order. Obviously, because it was filed under seal it would not be available to you in any way except if improperly provided to you by a party. You can choose to ignore that if you like; I assume you are going too anyway but thought you ought to be forewarned.

The rest of your email is irrelevant to the matter at hand.

Regards,

Dan Backer, Esq.

The game was afoot.

Dan, these documents are not part of any discovery responses. And, if I'm not mistaken, the order only applies to responses to Kimberlin's request for discovery. Now, if you can provide me with a copy of the judge's order that specifically states THESE DOCUMENTS, all 300+ pages thereof, are covered by the Judge's order, I will comply and not publish.

Kindly send me a copy of the judge's October 5 order. We'll see if it matches the copy of the October 5 order I already have. And you have stated several things. First, you said you could not comment on the document I sent Walker. Then you said you had no way of knowing if it was part of the order. Now you are saying it IS part of the order? Can you try to keep your story straight for my benefit?

Thanks, Dan.

Bill

Conveniently, that's when Dan lost his power during the hurricane.

Power just went out and I need to conserve laptop and phone power (my phone being my router), so please save your emails until Wednesday, I will not be responding until then. Here's what I just finished:

Yes, they are (or at least, the one portion of one email I have seen). That document was provided in response to a request for production from Mr. Kimberlin that is part of Discovery and was filed under seal.

You are mistaken; the judge expressly ordered the seal on all documents. Again, his order is publically available. I don't have a digital copy and am not in my office, but attached is the transcript from the hearing.

Thus, any material we filed in response to Mr. Kimberlin's discovery request was filed under seal, should not be available to anyone other than parties, and if you are in possession of it that seems to indicate someone violated a judges' order.

I think you are mistaken in your notes. First, I said I would not comment, but since it appeared to me you would publish it anyway, I decided I should at least give you fair notice. At which point I said the content appeared to be from the discovery materials (to the extent of what I saw), and that is what I am saying now. I don't believe I ever said that I "had no way of knowing if it was part of the order".

Regards,

Dan Backer, Esq.

He sent a copy of the judge's order. I read it carefully, then responded.

Sorry to hear about your power. This storm is really one for the books. I hope you and yours are safe and your power is restored soon.

Back to the document you sent.

Here's what the judge actually says.

Starting with Page 15, line 4. He is speaking to Kimberlin.

"I am going to deny your motion generally, but I will grant it with regards to discovery so that any answers to interrogatories cannot — and the reason I do this is because I have to look at the overall nature of this suit."

Lines 9 through 16 talk about the purpose of such suits and the role of the court.

We resume with Line 17. Again, addressing BK.

"So, whenever you file an answer to an interrogatory, a request for a production of any documents or an answer to the request for admissions, then you may file that with a protective order. That is to be filed and placed in confidentiality. It will be for the eyes of counsel for the parties only and that material is not to be reproduced otherwise. It's to be used soley for the purpose of this allegation.*"*

I submit, sir, that you are playing fast and loose with the words the judge uttered and are counting on the fact that I am not a lawyer to be bamboozled by them. As I once spent a horrible year in my youth making extra money for the law firm of Cooke & Franke in Milwaukee, I have a better than lay understanding of legal wording.

What the judge is clearly saying here is, when BK files an answer to an interrogatory, or a request for the production of any documents, or the answer to any admissions, he MAY DO SO with a protective order. THAT — is to be filed and placed in confidentiality. The PROTECTIVE ORDER will be filed and placed in confidentiality and will be for the eyes of counsel for the parties only and is not to be reproduced otherwise.

Line 23, page 16, continuing to page 17.

...there are a lot of 1st Amendment rights this Court will not infringe on. I think I have the ability under the rules to protect the parties for the purpose of this litigation.

Then, on line 10, he says:

So, I'll extend this protection to the parties. This would apply to the defense as well, in terms of any discovery that's filed by the other side. I think the protective order should extend to any response — again, to interrogatories, to request for production of documents, requests for admissions.

Sir, if I had a nickel for every "response to interrogatories" I word processed for Cooke and Franke, I would be a wealthy man. Same for "response to request for documents" and "response to request for admissions." These protections, this gag order you are trying to enforce, does NOT apply to the documents actually produced, if any. IT APPLIES TO THE RESPONSE TO THE INTERROGATORIES, THE RESPONSE TO THE REQUEST FOR DOCUMENTS, THE RESPONSE FOR THE REQUEST FOR ADMISSIONS — NOT the actual documents turned over in the discovery process.

Given the fact that Walker blogs EVERY DAY about this case... given the fact that every friend of Walker's writes about this case every day, given the fact that Walker is using this case to portray himself as a victim and is using this case as a cash cow to milk as he sees fit, you will pardon me if I use my brain to interpret what the judge actually SAID, as opposed to what you want me to THINK he said.

Like I said, that might work with the chicks. But not me.

Good luck with the storm.

Bill

He wasn't buying it. At least, I don't think he was.

Read the rest of the transcript. Judge clearly applies it to bob. And that's what the order say.

Dan. I read the entire transcript. I quoted directly from it. Who is "Bob"? I assume you meant "both". I stand by what I sent you. What's more, your concern for my well-being is touching. If only President Obama had as much concern for Mitt Romney when he stumbled on the Libya situation, warning him in the debate, "Uh, Governor, you don't want to say what you are about to say," instead of just saying, "Proceed, Governor."

Thank you for your concern. I am convinced I am correct, as I know how to read. Show me something that...

A. Proves the DOCUMENTS produced by a request for discovery are under the order, not just the request itself, andB. These documents were PROVIDED by a request for discovery — i.e., a copy of the document specifically asking for these documents.

Other than that, I will repeat my well wishes and bid you good night.

Bill

Finished reading your email. you did indeed read the transcript, but you interpret it in a manner wholly inconsistent with law. A request for production is a request to produce a document. The document you possess is a document produced in response to that request. It is therefore protected by the judges express words and the order issued, that anything filed in response to discover be sealed. To say that a document product in response to the request for production is not covered by the seal on such responses because it is a document is patently absurd. There is no other possible responsive answer to a request for production other than a document.

I encourage you to read the text of the order and the relevant rule of the Supreme Court. Beyond that, if you want to self-justify breaching the order, that is your perogative, but it is still breach no matter how you choose to justify it.

Sent from my iPhone, please excuse any typos.

He was not about to concede. I hadn't said the right words yet.

Dan, I know this would be easier for you if I was some dimwit who didn't know anything about the law and hadn't worked closely with and for lawyers in the past. The "response to a request for production of documents" referred to in the Judge's order does NOT consist of the turned over documents. A "response to a request for production of documents" is a legal form, and that form is what the Judge has ordered sealed.

Here are some typical legal "response to a request for production of documents."

In the future, please reserve stupid responses to stupid people.

Thank you again for the concern for my well-being. It's really touching that you put my interests ahead of those of your client. You're a sweetheart.

I attached three typical "Responses to Requests for Production of Documents".

THESE are the documents covered by the order. Not any documents turned over. And Backer had not even tried to prove that the documents I had were turned over in discovery. He had no answer for that. So he said this instead.

I've responded already, and frankly that's it. I've given you the information you requested and if you choose to ignore it in favor of your own unique interpretation of the law, that's your choice.

Sent from my iPhone, please excuse any typos.

That required a rebuttal.

Actually, it's not unique. Walker violates this order on a daily basis. So does his pal, WJJ Hoge.

Nite!

Bill

Then, I went to bed. This was waiting for me in the morning.

Good morning.

Sir, notwithstanding your extensive experience in the legal profession, you are clearly mistaken in this regard; which you would understand where you actually an attorney.

That said, you are going to do whatever you want anyway – as you always were – and if you feel the need to self-justify your actions by making up bizarre readings of the law to pretend you are somehow not facilitating the violation of a court order, so be it. But there is no need to share it with me.

Have a good day.

Regards,

Dan Backer, Esq.

Oh, the biting, cutting sarcasm.

How odd that the two attorneys I have consulted strongly disagree with you. But then, try to get two attorneys to agree on anything, right, Dan?

Again, your concern for my well-being when, if what I am doing would in fact benefit your client, is touching, Dan. If it were me, I might be inclined to let someone stumble into making a critical error that would assist my client into winning a case. But the fact that you continue to worry about my well-being, well sir, it reaffirms my faith in the legal community and the overall GOODNESS of those with a right wing point of view. Thank you. Thank you. Thank you.

Be well.

Bill Schmalfeldt

He responded with two words that told me my point had been made and I had proven my case.

You're Welcome.

Now, if Dan Backer and his big, right wing Republican nut sack wants to drag my nearly 58-year old, has had Parkinson's disease, can't walk without help, Porky Pig stuttering ass down to Virginia, fine. I'll testify. I will read each and every word of these documents into the record. And I gave my word to not reveal my source, so if the judge wants that, he can put me in the jail's hospital ward. In the meantime, we'll take this regional bit of fooferaw and turn it into a fucking NATIONAL STORY about how the lawyer for a right wing Islamophobe, suing someone for making him stand behind his written hatred with his actual name, jailed a Parkinson's sufferer for defending his First Amendment right to print publicly available information,

That'll be a *good* story!

One power lawyers (the arrogant ones, anyway) think they have over a citizen with average intelligence is that they have some sort of bestowed-by-degree ability to read arcane legal rules and regulations and make sense of them. The REALLY arrogant ones will try to convince the layperson that the words on the paper mean the exact OPPOSITE of what they say!

For instance.

2006 Code of Virginia § 18.2-178 – Obtaining money or signature, etc., by false pretense

It's a nice law. A good law. A simple law that basically says it's against the law to ask people to give you money for reasons that are not true. Like when rot-toothed pornographer Lee Stranahan asked people to donate to his PayPal account to help him move out of his nice house in Dallas because I published his address, which he had published online himself dozens of times. Not only was there no threat, Stranahan never moved. Therefore, anyone who gave him money to move to protect him from a threat that never existed, donated money under false pretenses.

But that's Texas. This is a Virginia law. So let's see if we can come up with a Virginia case for the purposes of discussion.

Hmmm…

I KNOW!

Let's say a lawyer is fired from his job as compliance counsel for a Health Care provider. This lawyer, according to the lawyer who actually notified him he was fired, did private work on business time in an effort to harass and stalk someone for no other reason than the person had been convicted of a crime 40 years earlier and was now, after paying his debt to society, working for progressive interests.

This lawyer plotted and planned with others, including a Los Angeles County Deputy District Attorney and a writer for a famous right wing smear blog, to come up with ways to link this progressive to other progressives and somehow implicate them in all manner of crimes. The lawyer, during company time, also provided legal services to a very, very, tiny, insignificant small time blogger who had a personal bone to pick with the progressive because he was the partner of a blog owner the little, bitty, too-small-to-be-seen-by-the-human-eye, insignificant blogger wanted to write for, but was denied because, well, he's a disgusting troll.

Now, along the way, the progressive activist, using entirely legal means, learns the identity of this lawyer, who blogs under a pen name to keep his actual identity hidden because he also ran an "everybody draw Mohammed" blog that drew national interest and righteous indignation from Islamic extremists and even Islamic moderates who believe images depicting the Prophet are blasphemous. In his "super secret blogger" identity, the lawyer indicated that he KNEW he was insulting Muslims, he ENJOYED insulting Muslims, and he INVITED angry Muslims to hunt him down and behead him — if they could.

When the progressive activist, through entirely legal means, determined the lawyer's actual identity, the lawyer had a mental meltdown. He wrote a long, pathetic letter to his employer explaining how everything bad that was happening to him was because of the progressive activist he was harassing, suing and stalking.

His employer didn't see it that way. They hired another lawyer to come in, kick out the blogging lawyer, and fumigate the stench of religious hatred from his tiny, cluttered office.

Humiliated, but never humbled, the bloggy lawyer refused to identify himself on his blog, even though the progressive activist published his actual name in court proceedings.

What the bloggy lawyer did, instead, was tell the readers of his blog that he lost his job due to terroristic threats made by the progressive activist. That the progressive activist had threatened his wife's life, his life, and had placed his coworkers in danger, he falsely claimed. And since he was without a job, would you be so kind as to hit the "donate" button on his blog so he can feed his wife and keep a roof over his head?

And the bloggy lawyer is not the ONLY one dangling from this precarious legal branch.

ANOTHER lawyer came along to DEFEND the bloggy lawyer. He and his company took over from the horribly failed, illegal and incompetent National Bloggers Club, founded by felon Ali Akbar, including board members such as noted right wing screech queen Michelle Malkin, when conservatives started to ask, "Hey! I donated! What are you doing with my MONEY?" And they NEVER got an answer.

So, the big right wing CORPORATE lawyer founded something called the **Bloggers Defense Team**, and HE is raising money and here is what HE says is the reason you should give him your hard earned kerblingy.

While (the progressive activist's) lawfare assault on (the bloggy lawyer)- which cost (the bloggy lawyer) his job, his reputation, and falsified criminal charges – is finally garnering media attention, (the progressive activist's) list of victims is still growing, and the stakes are becoming life and death.

Well, yeah... but it wasn't... um... that wasn't the reason why.... uh....

Those who believe in free speech must unite to defend the victims of (the progressive activist's) harassment, fight back against these sordid tactics, and pursue both (the progressive activist) and his allies and donors for this unlawful conduct and their knowing or tacit support.

And how would we do that, exactly?

But if we donate for the reasons you give on your website, we'd be donating... under...

FALSE PRETENSES!!!

NOW, TO THE POINT OF LAW.

The bloggy lawyer, **Aaron Walker,** was **NOT** fired because of a terroristic threat. He was fired, among other reasons, because the company he worked for did not want to be subjected to the anger of an outraged Islamic community for employing someone who blatantly, repeatedly, gleefully blasphemed the top prophet of their religion. They did not want such a person working for them. The lawyer his company brought in to dispense with him also cited his reckless disregard for his co-workers, gross negligence of his official duties, working on his blog and Kimberlin lawfare on company time, and his overall reckless behavior. So they fired him, as was their right.

Bottom line. Despite what Aaron Walker says on his blog, he was not fired because of Brett Kimberlin and terroristic threats. He was fired because he was a terrible employee and deserved to be fired.

The CORPORATE lawyer, **Dan Backer** of DB Capitol Strategies and RightSolutions, is raising money under the exact same false pretenses.

Therefore, to say that he needs your money because of terroristic threats by Brett Kimberlin is a lie. And raising money based on a lie falls under the auspices of Virginia Code, § 18.2-178 – Obtaining money or signature, etc., by false pretense.

On the face of it, it would seem that if anyone wanted to press charges against Aaron Walker and/or Dan Backer for violating this law, they would have an excellent case!

See... this is what I mean about lawyers and the fact that the arrogant ones think that law can only be deciphered by using a juris prudence degree as a seer stone — an umin and thummin, if you will...

Golly. You would think two smart lawyer fellers like Walker and Backer would be able to read a simple little law like Code of Virginia § 18.2-178.

See if this law seems difficult for you to comprehend.

A. If any person obtain, by any false pretense or token, from any person, with intent to defraud, money, a gift certificate or other property that may be the subject of larceny, he shall be deemed guilty of larceny thereof; or if he obtain, by any false pretense or token, with such intent, the signature of any person to a writing, the false making whereof would be forgery, he shall be guilty of a Class 4 felony.

B. Venue for the trial of any person charged with an offense under this section may be in the county or city in which (i) any act was performed in furtherance of the offense, or (ii) the person charged with the offense resided at the time of the offense.

Now, here is what a prosecutor would have to prove.

1. Did Aaron Walker receive money under false pretenses?

Anyone who donated to his "donate" button on his blog believing that he was fired because, as he put it, *"My wife and I have lost our jobs due to the harassment of convicted terrorist Brett Kimberlin, including an attempt to get us killed and to frame me for a crime carrying a sentence of up to ten years…"* then you donated under false pretenses.

He did *not* lose his job because of harassment of a convicted terrorist.

Brett Kimberlin did *not* attempt to get them killed.

Brett Kimberlin did *not* frame him for a crime carrying a sentence up to 10 years.

According to the lawyer who fired him, and you can read the entire letter *(first, the one written by Walker, then the back and forth between the lawyer Walker's employer hired to dispose of him and Walker)*, Walker was fired because of **HIS** actions, not those of anyone else. There is no evidence that Kimberlin harassed him. The "attempt to get him killed" turns out to be the fact that Kimberlin made Walker's actual name public, and the "crime carrying a sentence of up to ten years" comes from Walker's hamfisted grabbing of Kimberlin's iPad away from him in a courthouse hallway (because, Walker said, he thought Kimberlin had a scary BOMB in the iPad), resulting in an injury to Kimberlin's eye and an assault charge that was dismissed.

Again. **False pretenses.**

2. Did Dan Backer receive money under false pretenses?

Well, we assume Backer has seen the same documents we have, and now you have, and knows the actual reason given by Walker's employer for Walker's dismissal. So saying Walker was dismissed for any other reason would be *prima facie* (that means *on its face*) **FALSE PRETENSE!**

BACK TO THE SOURCE OF THE EVIL

Bill Schmalfeldt would just be a minor blogger waiting to die in a trailer in Maryland were it not for his attack on Ali Akbar, head of the National Bloggers Club, Inc. Read and be AMAZED by Schmalfeldt's rationale for attacking this good and Godly man!

There's a name we've hardly mentioned here, and it needs to be mentioned, Ali Abdul Razaq Akbar. The former ringleader, although it seems as if Hoge and Walker are pretty much calling the shots these days,

This would be a good place to take a look at some of the research I've done, with others, on Mr. Akbar.

It is a uniquely American story. Crime, punishment, redemption, success.

But in most success stories, there is clear documentation as to how the person rose to such a level of success. This story has holes one could drive a large truck through.

How does one go from being a convicted felon in 2007 to becoming a bright and rising young star of the Republican party in 2012... all before his probation even expired... without some help or financing or special love from... someone?

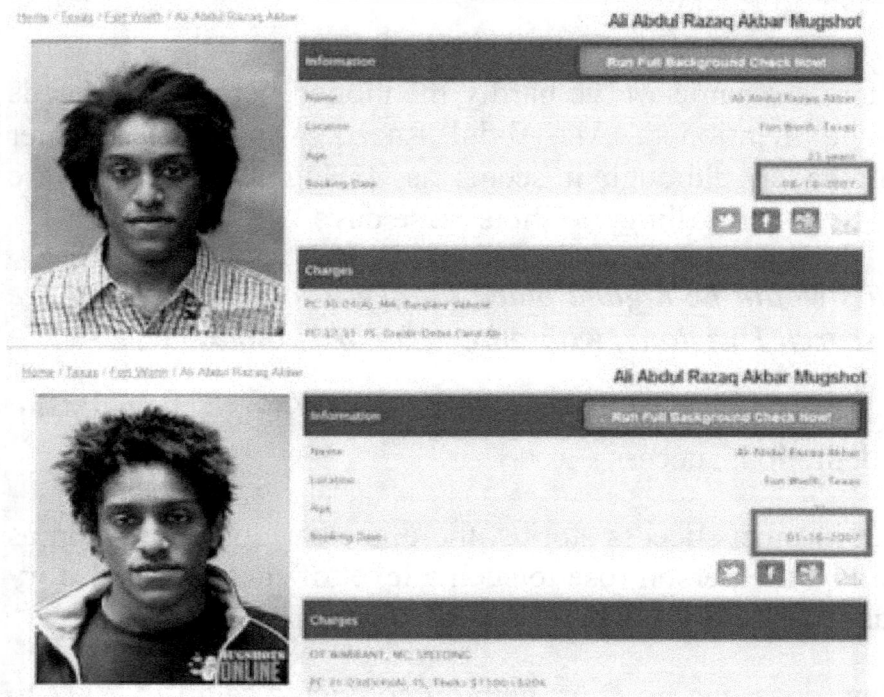

(Photos from Mugshots.com, used under Fair Use.)

Like all stories, this one has a beginning. We go back to late 2006 when a young man got into trouble with the law.

In November 2006, he was busted for stealing several items from a Fort Worth woman.

In early December, he broke into a van, stole a debit card, and attempted to use it.

In April 2008, Akbar took a guilty plea for the Debit Card fraud, was sentenced to four years probation and $400 restitution.

In between his illegal activities and his sentencing, he got involved in Republican Party politics.

In 2007, he became a member of the John McCain campaign. This is something he has both acknowledged and denied at different times.

On Dec. 17, 2007 -- four months before his sentencing -- Akbar ran afoul of the publisher of a website called "The Libertarian Republican" who wrote:

John McCain Campaign Staffer Ali Akbar from the Dallas/Ft. Worth area, is alleged to have discused using voter fraud techniques. This occured in an extended conference call within 1 month ago, with two other political operatives, one a volunteer for Ron Paul for President in Nevada. The staffer is in charge of a very key McCain for President campaign area. The staffer has been contacted by "higher-ups" in the McCain camp asking him to explain his statements.

More details emerging...

According to one sourve in the DFW area Akbar has had past problems with the law including credit card fraud. And that he might in fact be on parole.

The blog post continues:

Both Joey Dauben and Chuck Geshlider will be guests tonight at 8:00 pm cst on Blog Talk Radio's "Libertarian Politics Live." They will discuss the growing scandal involving McCain for President staffer Ali Akbar, and what they heard in the conference call. Call-in number is 646-915-9887. The show lasts one hour.

These days, Joey Dauben is appearing before a judge, facing charges of fraudulent use of identifying information while in jail over charges that he sexually abused a child. The abuse charge was dismissed. We told you this is a complicated story. After accusing Akbar, Dauben worked WITH Akbar.

After being released from the Tarrant County jail, Akbar moved a little bit south of the Dallas/Fort Worth Metro and found work as a web developer for the Ellis County Observer, for which Dauben was publisher. He soon ran into ethical problems in this job, as reported here.

Akbar was an executive editor and webmaster at the Observer, but was accused by proprietor Dauben of endorsing voter fraud tactics. But Akbar helped Dauben determine via IP address tracing certain posts that on the Observer that he says were made by his arch-enemy (John) Hoskins.

After signing his probation papers, Akbar lit off for South Georgia -- but not before telling a reporter for the Dallas Morning News in September 2008 that he was a student at the University of North Texas... which he was.

He was a student there, according to the registrar, for four months in 2005.

So, it was off to Georgia, to follow a rising star in the Republican Party. With no job, no visible means of support, and a felony conviction following him, what was a young

Republican going to do with himself and how would he make a life in this new environment.

Having decided, apparently, that Texas was now unfriendly turf, young Akbar decided to move to South Carolina to work for Ray McKinney a candidate who had pulled off a political shocker -- winning a Republican Straw Poll for the 2008 Presidential nomination.

With McKinney, Akbar discovered something he was good at... advocating for GOP candidates.

When McKinney lost the GOP nomination to another candidate in 2008, he worked for a tea party favorite in the New York 23th Congressional District. He supported Tea Party insurgent Bob Hoffman over the eventual winner, Democrat Bill Owens.

When the special election was over, Akbar went back to work with McKinney. In 2010, McKinney won the primary, and his opponent charged Akbar with unethical behavior.

So, he wasn't being paid. He had no money, as evidenced by the fact that he was evicted from his residence in Savannah in Feb. 2010.

He wasn't working for McKinney. He had no visible source of support. So, who was paying Akbar to travel to New York to harass the Democratic candidate? Who was paying for Akbar to stump for McKinney? Where did he live? Who paid the tab?

McKinney lost in the general election. Akbar decided to cut his losses and head back to Texas.

Somewhere along the way, Young Akbar met Republican superstar Karl Rove and RNC Chairman Ed Gillespie.

That's when Ali Akbar's star began to really shoot into the firmament.

You have a name that is as improbable for success in the American political arena as Barack Hussein Obama.

Ali Akbar.

Unlike the president, you're an ex-con with no education. You've had some success ingratiating yourself into the regional tea party scene with your work for two losing candidates. But now, you have no home, you have no job, you have no money. What do you do?

Well, according to blog entries, YouTube videos and other sources, you make friends with Karl Rove.

Now, all of a sudden you have money, star power and cache. You can start organizations like the Vice and Victory agency. You can support a candidate for the College Republican National Committee (who will ultimately be drubbed in the CRNC election). You can start holding meet and greets at the annual Conservative Political Action Committee (CPAC) annual meetings. You can dole out whiskey and cigars to politicians and pundits alike.

You can become a star.

There is no official record of when young Akbar met Rove or RNC Chairman Ed Gillespie. But in the accompanying video, he mentions working with them at the 2:17 mark.

And it's still 2011, then early 2012.

His probation for his debit card fraud wasn't even lifted until May 2, 2012.

By then, Akbar and his friends had formed a new fund, ostensibly created to help fund beleaguered blogger Aaron Walker, who was spending all his money and had lost his job because of his ongoing war of words with liberal activist Brett Kimberlin, who had spent time in prison after being convicted for the so-called "Speedway Bombings" in the 1970s.

It was at this point in his history that young Akbar caught the eye of two bloggers who read about this young man with raised eyebrows. One of these bloggers, "Breitbart Unmasked" first ran a series of stories about Akbar and his "National Bloggers Club," which was claiming 501(c)3 status, meaning they were telling their benefactors their deductions would be tax deductible.

Our blogging alter ego, The Liberal Grouch, personally contacted Akbar and put forward a simple request... something any legitimate 501(c)3 fundraiser can easily do. Provide your Employer Identification Number so we can check your status with the IRS.

Akbar, who tweets under the name @Ali, refused. Then he blocked The Liberal Grouch from his Twitter accounts and from commenting on the National Blogger's Club Facebook page.

Working together, Breitbart Unmasked and The Liberal Grouch informed their readers about Akbar's criminal past by posting his mugshots and screen captures of the legal documents filed in the case. Akbar responded with a whiny post on his Facebook page, claiming that he was not the active criminal in the complaint -- that he was just providing a friend with a ride and the friend had the stolen debit card and tried to use it.

The legal documents, however, proved that to be untrue. While most of his conservative blogger friends gladly lapped up the lie, there were a few, to their credit, who were not willing to do so and called on Akbar to step down as president of the National Blogger's Club. Akbar refused.

The Liberal Grouch personally called an agent at the IRS, provided Akbar's name, the name of the organization, the other members listed on the "Board of Directors", and was told by the IRS agent that there was no record of the National Blogger's Club ever registering as a 501(c)3 agency.

The Club changed their website, removing the claim to be a tax-exempt organization, instead referring to themselves as "non-profit."

Around this time, Karl Rove made a disastrous appearance on the Greta Van Sustren show on Fox News. Blogger "The Legal Schnauzer," working with other informants, interpreted Rove's bizarre behavior on the show as "panic" that he was about to be outed as a gay man.

Karl Rove is having a bisexual affair with the president of a conservative bloggers' group, and concern about being outed sparked Rove's falsehood-filled diatribe last week on Greta Van Susteren's Fox News program.

Rove's lover is Ali Akbar, president of the National Bloggers Club, an umbrella group that grew from the activism of the late right-wing publisher and pundit Andrew Breitbart. A left-leaning Web site called Breitbart Unmasked recently disclosed that Akbar has a criminal record that includes convictions for credit-card fraud, theft, and burglary.

The stunning allegations about Rove and Akbar are included in a letter sent yesterday from Alabama attorney Dana Jill Simpson to Robert Bauer, counsel for President Barack Obama's 2012 re-election campaign. The letter also includes an appeal for a presidential pardon on behalf of former Alabama Governor Don Siegelman.

This allegation was bolstered by the revelation of an image of Akbar taken from a screen cap from the smartphone application for gay men looking for companionship resembling Akbar, looking for "a masculine chill bud to hang with."

The more Akbar chose to ignore the legitimate questions posed by bloggers, the more The Liberal Grouch (an impish sort) decided to rattle Akbar's cage.

In late June, he posted an item on his Zazzle store that contained this picture. It is Akbar, wearing an Obama mask, waving $20 bills in someone's face. The Liberal Grouch added some word balloons and other items to the photo, and used it as an image on items he was selling on his Zazzle store to raise money for Parkinson's disease research.

The next day, the Grouch received an e-mail from the Zazzle Content Management Team telling him they were removing the item because it violated someone's "intellectual property rights."

"Whose rights," the Grouch responded.

The response was stunning and telling all at the same time.

The Liberal Grouch blinked in disbelief at the e-mail response he had received to his questions to the Zazzle Management Team, which had just informed him they were removing an image of Ali Akbar, wearing a Barack Obama mask, waving money in the photographer's face.

KARL ROVE?

How in God's name can Karl Rove claim intellectual property rights over the image? He's not pictured. His full name is not used. Unless he has copyrighted the word "Rove" or "Mister Rove," the only way he could claim intellectual property rights would be...

...if he took the photo?

The Grouch rolled that idea around in his head. Look at the setting. It seems to be a private room somewhere. The flash indicates the camera, most likely a smart phone, was being held at a level below and in front of Akbar... about belt level.

"Oh, lord," he thought.

The Grouch tried to contact Akbar via Twitter to get a comment. Still blocked. He wrote to Karl Rove's contact info on his website. No reply. He and other bloggers poured over the issue for about a month, but no new info came out...

Except for the fact that Rove suddenly, days after his alleged "gay panic" attack on the Greta Van Sustren show on Fox, dashed off to Italy where he married his long time female friend, some say his "beard", Karen Johnson. Also along for the honeymoon fun, Rove's pal, casino owner and contributor, Steve Wynn. But who doesn't take a good pal along for the ride on a fancy, Italian honeymoon?

Further poking and prodding at Akbar produced no results and the story went cold.

Until yesterday. We were contacted by Alabama investigative reporter Lori Moore. While investigating the Rove-connected "railroading" of former Alabama governor Don Siegelman, she ran across the Grouch's story about having his Zazzle image pulled down at the demand of Karl Rove.

She used the same contact form the Grouch had used in July. But instead of ignoring her, as they had him, they responded within hours.

So, the Grouch responded to the Rove spokesperson.

Ms. Tahilramani:

She got her research and information from me. I am the person who had an item removed from Zazzle at the demand of Karl Rove & Company as it "infringed on your intellectual property rights".

Attached in the e-mail correspondence I had with Zazzle, a copy of the photo in question, and a screen cap of my attempt to contact your office for an explanation. I had intended to donate the profits from the sale of an item I created to the National Parkinson Foundation. They provide services to people like myself and our caregivers. I am a retired government writer, living with PD for more than 12 years now. Rove's decision is the same thing as taking money away from people with Parkinson's disease. Now, I know Rove and Company does not want to be seen as a company that stands against the funding of a cure for Parkinson's — that would be horrible publicity for Mr. Rove and might disturb his new marriage, a happy occurrence taking place shortly after a published news account that suggested Mr. Rove might not be so inclined as to marry a person of the opposite sex. So, I know I can count on a quick, ON THE RECORD, response from you as to the reasons this photograph was claimed as Mr Rove's intellectual property.

I hope I can count on your speedy response, as I have waited for months to hear something, and you responded to Ms. Moore's inquiry the same day as she asked.

BTW: A little lesson in journalism. You need to get the reporter's AGREEMENT that something will be off the record BEFORE you share the information.

Now... please... once and for all so we can put this matter to rest... what was Rove's "intellectual property interest" in this photo?

She responded with the exact same information she sent to Ms. Moore.

I am not sure where you are getting your research and information but we do not request the removal of anything for which we do not hold rights to.

This riled up the Grouch, but good.

Sheena. I got my information from Zazzle, which says Karl Rove ordered the removal of the image. I have provided you with the image. I have provided you with the letter from Zazzle. Are you saying Zazzle lied? Or are you claiming Karl Rove owns the intellectual rights to the image? You need to clear this up, Sheena. Standard, pat answers will not do here. The facts are, Zazzle removed the image. They explained they were contacted by Karl Rove and Company which said they owned the intellectual property to the image.

Your answer does not say you did NOT order the removal of the image. So, I will take your response and report it as the image WAS removed at the request of Karl Rove because Karl DOES have intellectual property rights to the image, because, according to Sheena A. Tahilramani, Chief of Staff of Karl Rove & Company, "we do not request the removal for anything we do not hold rights to."

Will that be factually correct?

The game was afoot.

Bill,

As I said, we do not request the removal of anything for which we do not own the rights to.

My best suggestion is that you contact Zazzle and clear up any miscommunication with them.

Appreciate you reaching out and I hope you're able to successfully resolve the issue.

The Grouch felt he was being played with as the Rove flack parsed her words. So, he sent her the actual image that had taken down.

OK, did Rove and Company demand removal of THIS image? This is the image that I was marketing to raise money for PD. Zazzle was as clear as clear could be. The item was the intellectual property of Karl Rove. Are you saying that Rove & Company did not order the removal of THIS image? Does Mr. Rove claim intellectual property rights over the word "Rove" or "Mr. Rove"? Has he copyrighted that word?

I just want to be absolutely clear. The image I've showed you so far was not on the items I was trying to sell. THIS image was. So, yes or no. Did Rove and Company contact Zazzle, as they clearly stated in their e-mail to me, and demand that this image, the one attached to this e-mail, be removed from my Zazzle account because Rove had "intellectual property rights"?

This time, a clear, non-parsed response.

Bill,

We did not request the removal of this particular item or image.

Please contact Zazzle if you have any additional questions or concerns.

So. Somebody is lying. Either Zazzle lied about who demanded the image be removed, or the Rove flack is lying today.

We've written to the Content Management Team at Zazzle to see if they can shed any further light on this issue. We will share their response.

But none of this sheds any real light on how someone can literally go from the gutter, to being quoted by columnists like Dan Weigel of Slate as being a mover and shaker in the young Republican stratosphere. With no money, no visible means of support, only a semester of college and a felony conviction, who picked up the tab? Who paid his way? Who placed him in this position of power? And why won't he answer these questions? We don't believe Zazzle had any reason to lie about Rove demanding the item be removed from the Zazzle story. So, why is Rove lying about it? Is he lying about it? Or does Zazzle have some inexplicable reason to lie?

Why did Karl Rove dash off and get married to a female friend he has known for years mere days after published reports suggested he was having an affair with Ali?

So many questions, too few answers. But interesting nonetheless.

One thing you can always count on from a Conservative -- and that's being consistent. If they hate you today, they will hate you tomorrow, next month, next year and forever. Until they don't anymore.

Such is the case of right wing, Tea party darling and GOP operative Ali Abdul Razaq Akbar. We shared several stories about him yesterday concerning his baffling, inexplicable and meteoric rise from being a convicted felon to becoming the brightest star in the young Republican establishment, all without benefit of a college education, any visible means of support or anything to work with other than his good looks and charm and "very close friendship" with Karl Rove -- who is well known inside the beltway for his enjoyment of young lads with good looks and charm and political skills that can be used to his benefit, among other things.

Well, through 2010 and 2011, Akbar was working his young hiney off for Tea party candidates. He supported Newt Gingrich.

He supported Tim Pawlenty.

But the one guy he could not, WOULD not support...

That pretend conservative, the notorious flip flopper, the RINO (Republican in Name Only)...

Willard Mitt Romney.

A November 6, 2011 blurb in the New York Post told the story.

A movement is bubbling in DC among conservative operatives and talking heads who don't think Mitt Romney has what it takes to beat President Obama. Freedom Works' Tabitha Hale, Gaypatriot.org blogger Bruce Carroll, Townhall's John Hawkins, Tea Party activist Tiffiny Ruegner and GOP political consultants Matt Mackowiak and Ali Akbar are launching NotMittRomney.com today as a grass-roots effort to oppose his nomination.

Grrrr! No way was Ali Akbar going to just SIT there on his smooth, Republican rear end and allow this flip flopper to get the nomination.

They even threw together a 30-sec ad to demand conservative voters nominate ANYONE but Mitt Romney.

We'd give you the URL's to these websites. But there's a problem. When you click them now, they take you directly to Mitt Romney's campaign page.

WHAT? WHAT? Did the nefarious Romney somehow hack into Ali's Vice and Victory agency and do some sort of evil redirect so that people righteously angry about Romney's assured ascendency to the GOP nomination would no longer have a place to vent.

No.

You see, Conservatives are good at something else, too.

When they are told to, they get in line and support who they are told to. All that other stuff you read? Fuhgeddabouddit. They're kind of like Mormons that way. After over 100 years of being told that Black people could not be priests in the Church of Jesus Christ of Latter Day Saints, after proclamations by none other than Brigham Young, the successor to the church's founder Joseph Smith, Jr., included in sermons such as:

"..Shall I tell you the law of God in regard to the African race? If the white man who belongs to the chosen seed mixes his blood with the seed of Cain, the penalty, under the law of God, is death on the spot. This will always be so." – JoD: vol.10 p. 110: (March 8, 1863)

After the Quorum of the Twelve had a sudden "revelation" directly from God himself, they decided that God was telling them Black people were OK now, and Mormons should just disregard all the previous teachings of the church in that regard, according to Apostle Bruce R. McConkle.

Forget everything that I have said, or what President Brigham Young or President George Q. Cannon or whomsoever has said in days past that is contrary to the present revelation. We spoke with a limited understanding and without the light and knowledge that now has come into the world.... We get our truth and our light line upon line and precept upon precept. We have now had added a new flood of intelligence and light on this particular subject, and it erases all the darkness and all the views and all the thoughts of the past. They don't matter any more.... It doesn't make a particle of difference what anybody ever said about the Negro matter before the first day of June of this year.

So, apparently, the people who could not stand the idea of Romney as their nominee had a similar revelation.

As for Akbar, he's full speed ahead on Romney now!

Never mind what he said before.

Just check his Twitter postings (which we are actually blocked from but can still read through nefarious means).

Ali A. Akbar @ali Romney on FRC shooting: 62 words, 4 hours ago. Obama via Carney/press pool report via @TPM: 10 words, just now. Biden asserted that the President of the United States would be in #Chains if he lost to Governor Romney. Entirely racist comment.

Ali A. Akbar @ali @ViralRead: Romney Surrogate Responds to @Soledad_OBrien's violation of journo ethics: http://akbar.co/RdZrRz

Ali A. Akbar @ali Bizarrely cool quote from @MittRomney: "His strategy is to smash America apart and cobble together 51 pieces."

Ali A. Akbar @ali On the ground in Ohio: THE CHILLICOTHE ADDRESS: Romney's Best Speech of the Campaign by @rsmccain http://akbar.co/JWu4ah

Ali A. Akbar @ali @Sammy4Liberty Has he endorsed Romney? Has he told people to vote for the Republican ticket?

Akbar clung to his belief that Romney would win the 2012 presidential election until well after all the networks had declared Obama the winner.

Such dedication.

Akbar's partner, right hand man and #1 lickspittle has the distinction of being listed as a member of a hate group by the Southern Poverty Law center.

R. Stacy McCain is, in my opinion, one of the most blindly hate-filled people I've ever had the misfortune to come into contact with.

Before I got involved with this band of thugs, a Google search of my name would have revealed my work with Parkinson's disease awareness and fund raising. You would have seen links to my various blogs and satirical writing. Now, I am a deranged cyberstalker with an anal rape fixation.

The person most responsible for this Google bombing of my name and reputation is a weasel-faced, grey-toothed, hat wearing racist and misogynist named Robert Stacy McCain. He runs a little blog called "The Other McCain," where he deals in right wing rumor-mongering and soft-core porn.

McCain has written, God, I've lost count of how many articles about what an insignificant speck of humanity I am, unimportant, not worthy of his time or effort, or thousands and thousands of inches of column space on his blog.

Let's not delve that far into the fact that the Southern Poverty Law Center has designated McCain as belonging to a racial hate group, the white supremacist "neo-Confederate League of the South", a pro-secessionist organization that SPLC classifies as a hate group for its defense of segregation and slavery.

Let's deal with his rat-like personality and the hatred that oozes from every pore on his body.

Witness an e-mail he sent me in July 2013.

I refer to it as "5,000 Words of Hate.

His words are in plain text. Mine are **bold, italic**.

Mr. Schmalfeldt: You seem to think you deserve attention, but when you get the kind of attention you deserve, you don't seem to appreciate it very much. ***I deserve to be harassed by a drunken racist who can't get a real job writing for a real news organization***? You threaten and harass people, and if they ignore your threats, you accuse them of cowardice. ***I don't harass people. I ask questions. If they don't answer, I ask again. You used to know what that is. It's called "journalism."*** But when these people take notice of your bizarre and hateful conduct, you claim that you are a victim, that they have harassed or otherwise wronged you. ***I would call being deemed a pedophile by Ali Akbar bizarre and hateful. Wouldn't you?*** Perhaps there is some rational explanation for the notorious pattern of your online behavior, but damned if I can imagine what that might be. ***You start out with a false assumption that I am notorious and bizarre, you establish*** *it in your mind as truth, and you filter your every perception through that filter of your own creation.* Even if you were, as some suspect, being paid by Brett Kimberlin to stalk his targeted enemies and subject them to mental anguish — to provoke, annoy or intimidate them — your actions are either ineffective or self-defeating. *What kind of idiot would Brett Kimberlin be to pay someone to stalk and harass people when his chief objective, as far as I can tell, is to be left alone?* Your behavior, if done in Kimberlin's service, only further harms Kimberlin's reputation, because what kind of monster would hire such a monster as you? *And again, here we are operating through the filter you created, the filter you say is true because, well, you say so. You don't know me. You've never met me. And you never describe a single act I've done in my life that qualifies for the libelous term of "monster."* Because it has not been conclusively proven that you are employed or sponsored by Kimberlin, *and it won't be because I am not* then I have no choice but to suppose that you have been acting independently and of your own volition since you began cyberstalking Aaron Walker in June 2012. *By cyberstalking, of course, you mean the same process a journalist employs. Asking questions and expecting answers.* Therefore, by a process of elimination – deductive logic, Occam's Razor, etc. – this leads to exactly one explanation: YOU'RE CRAZY. *Faulty logic seems to be your specialty, Mr. McCain.*

Daft. Bonkers. Kooky. Bats in the belfry.

A few fries short of a Happy Meal. *(Name calling is fun, right Rummy?)*

Recall if you can, sir, the first time your name appeared on this blog. Don't bother looking it up, because I have not forgotten. It was Sept. 4, 2012, the day I left to cover the Democratic National Convention in Charlotte, N.C., in a post that included this:

Arrogant sociopathic punks think they can go around threatening people and if you dare say a word back to them, you're the bad guy.
Speaking of punks, an obscure talentless assclown named Bill Schmalfeldt is threatening to sue Aaron Walker. *(I don't recall making such a threat. I do recall Aaron Walker assuming a threat had been made, but let's face it. This is the guy who thought "Beware the Ides of March" was a death threat.)*

You may follow that link to Patterico – explaining threats against Lee Stranahan and Brandon Darby and the producers of Occupy Unmasked, threats that made headlines in the Hollywood Reporter — and to Aaron Walker's Allergic2Bull blog about your "Liberal Grouch" persona:

First off, my accusation was based on a series of tweets that Occupy Rebellion and Liberal Grouch — who are in constant contact — tweeted out. These are documented over at Joe Brooks' blog here and here. LG doesn't deny that he said these things and so he is angry at me for… drawing a conclusion about what he said that he doesn't like.
(Constant contact? What does that mean? We have a hot line? We exchange e-mails every day? Every now and then I get an e-mail? What does Aaron Walker know about how often I hear from Occupy Rebellion?)

You can read Aaron's blog post of Monday, Sept. 3, 2012, and see the evidence he provides of the association between yourself and "Occupy Rebellion," and what you wrote about Lee Stranahan's wife:

What I wrote about Lee Stranahan's wife, if you are referring to the fact that Lee used to at least attempt to sell her sex for a bottom dollar price of $290 if you were willing to come to the studio and $650 for a two-hour "session" if she came to your apartment to "deliver prints" has the unfortunate quality of being true and undisputed by Mr. Stranahan. It is backed up by screen caps of Mr. Stranahan's websites from the time. They live a different life now. Good. But it is an established fact that Lee would let you get naked with his wife if the price was right, and he has never denied it to my knowledge.

The blurred URL — was that a link to Lee Stranahan's home address? *Beats me. His address is a matter of public record and was all over the internet before I even knew of the guy. HE put it there. Not me.*

What did Lee Stranahan ever say or do to you, Mr. Schmalfeldt, to deserve such atrociously menacing behavior? Did you think that Lee Stranahan had no friends who would object to this? *Shall we start with the time Lee Stranahan sent cops to my house on a story that evolved over the days to my personally threatening to rape his wife, then his kids, then him? Then that story evolved into my supporting Occupy Rebellion's threat to rape his wife, his kids and then him? And how he took to Pay Pal to raise money so he could move in terror from his present location because of Bill Schmalfeldt and his horrible rape threat? A threat from a man who would have to ask his wife to drive him the 1,400 miles to Dallas. A wife who would likely ask the reason for such a trip and would probably not agree to take me to Dallas to rape Mr. or Mrs. Stranahan or their lovely children?*

Did you think that you could send such a message on Twitter and no one except your hateful sympathizers would notice it? Did it not occur to you, that in publicly associating yourself with a digital terrorist like Occupy Rebellion, *(and see, we are operating through your stained "truth filter" again. You SAY she is a digital terrorist, therefore she IS a digital terrorist)* that you were thereby forfeiting any presumption that you were acting in good faith?

Notice, Mr. Schmalfeldt, that I just called Occupy Rebellion a "digital terrorist," without fear of any legal consequence, because I know this:Sockpuppets can't sue for libel. One cannot defame a secretive menace who hides behind a pseudonymous Internet account. (*Which explains Kimberlin Unmasked.*) And given the close association between Occupy Rebellion and the terroristic threats against Lee Stranahan, Brandon Darby and others, who knows what an investigation of those e-mails and Twitter messages might discover? *But until such time as there is an ACTUAL investigation, you choose to pretend one has actually been concluded and will report its results as if they actually existed. Right?*

"We'll be legitimately raping Brandon Darby and Lee Stranahan for the next several days while they are tied up with the movie premier at the RNC," reads an email from occupyaunmasked2012@gmail.com. The email includes Darby's and Stranahan's cell phone numbers. *That's nice. And it has nothing to do with me.*

One tweet reads, "While @Shanahan is in Tampa this week, should Texas rapists be told where to find his wife since he supports the rape of everyone else?" *So, Occupy Rebellion has a call sheet of "the Texas Rapists" to activate at her command? She was writing about Stranahan's penchant for outing the name of rape victims and general slut-shaming. Was she over the top? Yeah. And I told her so at the time.*

"My wife is home with our four kids and freaked out," Stranahan told The Hollywood Reporter. "She's sick to her stomach." *But not that Stranahan has a flair for being a "drama queen" or anything.*

My point is that no sane, decent, honest, law-abiding person would associate themselves with persons responsible for such terroristic actions. But you did, didn't you, Mr. Schmalfeldt? *Again, through your beer-stained filter, you have acted as judge and jury and declared her actions "terroristic." And you operate on the premise that your assumptions are proven in a court of law, therefore they are true. But you do not have the luxury of deciding what is true and what is not, Mr. McCain. That is a question for a jury, not a disgraced, racist journalist, identified personally by the Southern Poverty Law Center as being a pernicious racist.*

A claim of defamation requires the demonstration of actual harm to the reputation of the plaintiff and of bad motives (mala fides) on the part of the defendant. A notorious criminal like Charles Manson cannot sue for defamation, because he has no good reputation that could be harmed. And a journalist reporting on Manson's crimes does not have bad motives for informing the public of such a criminal menace. But as my editors taught me long ago, truth is an absolute defense against any claim of libel: "Just get the facts right, and they can't touch you." *Well, try getting the facts right. Once.*

Ironic Justice for Occupy Rebellion

To describe Occupy Rebellion (hereafter OR) as a "digital terrorist" is simply a statement of fact, a vivid description based upon observation. However, as I say, sockpuppets can't sue for libel, and the OR account was recently deleted – poof! – and if you don't know why, Mr. Schmalfeldt, I certainly do. Some of OR's erstwhile allies in the "Anonymous" movement had become sick and tired of her obnoxious bullshit, and were ready to "patch" and "dox" her – to connect her online persona to her real-life name, and to make public her name, address, etc., so as to subject her to harassment at home and at work. *Whatever. That is OR. That is not me. I haven't been in contact with OR for months. And when we WERE in contact, it was a sporadic thing, where I was included in e-mails sent to others as well.*

This kind of terroristic activity — the implicit intimidation of what a swarming mob of online crazies might do to someone who is threatened with "doxing" — is not something any decent person can endorse, but it's what OR and her friends were glad to see inflicted on Aaron Walker,

Patrick "Patterico" Frey and other of their targets. So perhaps some will perceive an ironic justice in OR's misfortune. *Oh, spare me. Patrick Frey published the social security number and private medical information of Nadia Naffe, a woman who did him no harm. The interwebs are FULL of pages of right wing mental cases "Doxing" left wingers so spare me the sturm und drang.*

Occupy Rebellion is gone, Mr. Schmalfeldt, and so that relatively high-traffic Twitter account can no longer promote your harassing messages. *Again, I don't write harassing messages. I reply to people who harass me. Again, this is truth, unfiltered through your filter, Mr. McCain. Look at the top of this column. All within the past 12 hours. But I'm the harasser?*

This has deprived you of a hitherto valuable assistance in your campaigns against Walker, Stranahan, et al., which means you are back to the status I first described on Sept. 4 of last year when, at the end of a 954-word post, I called you an "obscure assclown." *Again, the assumption that I have a "campaign" against Walker, Stranahan, et. al. If anything, they have a campaign against me, as evidenced by their failed attempts to put me in jail for the mere act of trying to write stories about them.*

This I intended not as a mere insult, but as a statement of fact: You are obscure — an insignificant and unpopular nobody, which is why I hadn't paid any attention to you prior to September 2012 — and you are quite nearly the textbook definition of an assclown. *I asked you this before. If I am "obscure," why are you fixated on me? Why have you written so many stories and Twitter posts with the sole intention of defaming me? Why is it that a Google search of my name comes back with story after story written by R. Stacy McCain about my being a "deranged cyberstalker" as if it were true? Why is Walker fixated on me? Why is Hoge fixated on me? Why is it your seeming sword duty to destroy me? What harm have I caused you, Walker or Hoge?*

This is a compound word combining the meaning of "ass" — stupid and/or obnoxious — and "clown," a laughably incompetent person. If there were an Encyclopedia of Internet Pests, the entry defining "assclown" would end with a notation: "See also, Bill Schmalfeldt." *Blah, blah, blah.*

That Sept. 4, 2012, entry was not about you, Mr. Schmalfeldt, but rather about an e-mail I had received from Barrett Brown, my response to which was quoted in its entirety, a few excerpts of which I now call to your attention:

(Snip. I am not Barrett Brown. Irrelevant.)

The point is, the sound advice I gave Barrett Brown could apply equally to you, Mr. Schmalfeldt: "Spare me your lawsuit threats . . . you are traveling a road to destruction."

I don't believe I have threatened you with a lawsuit, Mr. McCain. Yet. But stand by.

Your threat of legal action was received, after you had sent obtuse messages on Twitter last week, hinting at all the terrible things that were about to happen to me — because this is your standard motif: "Beware, all ye whom

Schmalfeldt hates! Dreadful harm shall befall you! Be afraid! Be very afraid!"

Ali Akbar has replied at length to this threat, but my own response can be summarized in two words: Fuck you.

Yes. He called me a pedophile.

The advice my editors gave me long ago was simple: "If someone calls you to complain about a story, you should be polite, but the minute they mention 'libel' or otherwise threaten legal action, the conversation is over. Give them the name of our lawyers and tell them not to contact the newsroom again, as this is now a legal matter."

I'm giggling at the thought of you being "polite" in any interaction with a liberal.

Now, if the person is serious and the lawyers say "correct" or "retract," you follow their legal advice — that's what lawyers are for — but in nearly all cases, a threat of a lawsuit is merely that, a threat, an idiot's attempt to intimidate honest people into silence.

I am not an idiot, Mr. McCain. And I have said time and time again, please! Write whatever you want. Just make sure it's provably true and don't use any images I own.

We shall see how serious you are, Mr. Schmalfeldt, about pursuing your claims of copyright violation, and I'll let lawyers offer advice to Pundit Syndication LLC about whether my understanding of "fair use" is more accurate than yours. John Hoge, whom you have targeted with similar threats, seems certain of his own rights under "fair use" doctrine, but I'm not a lawyer and am unable to judge his case.

You certainly have no problem being a judge/jury and rendering verdicts on things you have no knowledge about. Why stop now?

As for your own understanding (of law or anything else), sir, I am quite certain it is impaired by the fact that YOU'RE CRAZY. *(You're a psychiatrist now?)*

Crackers. Psycho. Loopy. Off your rocker. Nuttier than a Snickers bar. *(Again with the name calling, eh, you brain-hardened sot?)*

Your claims of copyright infringement, insofar as they are not merely a delusional side-effect of your evident mental disorder, are clearly a continuation of the demonstrable pattern of obnoxious online behavior that first drew my attention to you in September 2012. *Defending my copyright is a sign of delusion?*

You cannot claim defamation, for I have not defamed you. *Ah, but you have. You have made countless negative claims about me that are not substantiated by fact. But nothing like Mr. Akbar calling me a pedophile yesterday.* You cannot claim harassment, because I have not harassed you. *Tell that to Mr. Hoge. He claims a hashtag mention is me harassing him. And again, I divert your limited attention to the top of this post.* So instead now you claim copyright infringement and, as I say, we shall see what the law says about that claim if, in fact, you seriously intend to pursue that claim. *I will fight to claim my ownership of things I own.* My hunch is that you have no such intention, *you've been wrong about SO many things.* but have merely threatenedlegal action, hoping to intimidate our web hosting provider, and to use this implausible threat as a basis for calling me a "thief."

To repeat the earlier summary: Fuck you. *(That actually helps my case. Thank you.)*

The Game That Homey Does Not Play

You may wonder, Mr. Schmalfeldt, why I am sending this email to you, as I have hitherto avoided any direct communication with you. *(Preferring to rattle on about me in a defamatory fashion behind my back, like most cowards.)* I have on occasion written about your actions, but never have I written to you, even while you have repeatedly targeted me with your own hostile communications. *(To reply to your defamatory remarks written about me like the coward I believe you to be.)* The first time your photo appeared on this blog, was in November 2012, during Thanksgiving weekend when you sent me more than 200 harassing Twitter messages in a span of 48 hours. Rather than respond to on Twitter, I instead put up this blog post on Nov. 24:

(snip because irrelevant)

The answer is: Because I'm a journalist, covering a story — the story of how conservative bloggers have been harassed by an entity that has become colloquially known as "Team Kimberlin," an entity of which you, Bill Schmalfeldt, are very much an active part. *(Ah. The same reason I give for "harassing" the people you claim I "cyberstalk." But you get to claim it because — you. I don't get to claim it because – me. Perfectly sensible.)* I seldom block troll accounts on Twitter because, since I started covering this story in May 2012, most of the psychos who show up in my timeline screaming lunatic accusations at me are part of the online troll-swarm of which Kimberlin's associate Neal Rauhauser is generally acknowledged as the ringleader. I don't block them, because I want to keep tabs on what they're up to — they are part of the story — which is why I never blocked you.

And if you don't remember why you were threatening to call my wife (!) in November 2012, Mr. Schmalfeldt, I most certainly do: *(How is that a threat? If you won't answer a question, a journalist will take the next step and ask a person who knows the person. But please, Mr. McCain. Proceed.)* Last year, I moved out of Maryland and, not long before you started that particularly frenzied episode of harassment over the Thanksgiving holidays, I was informed that Neal Rauhauser had expressed interest in discovering where I'd moved. (Gee, I wonder why? Maybe Patrick Frey or Mike Stack could imagine a reason.) So when you started yammering at me on Twitter, making false claims that I had not moved from Maryland, I made three inferences:
Neal Rauhauser was behind it;
The purpose was to find out where I live; and
The excessively belligerent nature of your harassment was an attempt to get me to contact the police or otherwise seek legal action against you, hoping that I would thereby create a public record of my new address and then – boom! – I would have in effect doxed myself. *(Which is why I felt the need, as a journalist, to call your wife because I did not*

believe you were being honest. And despite the look of fear about the woman at the thought of what you might do to her for answering me, I figured she would be honest and tell me the truth about whether or not you had actually relocated or were just using your "fear" as a fund-raising excuse, seeing how well it worked for Stranahan.)

What part of "fuck you" do I need to explain, Bill? I knew very well, that late November weekend, that the Virginia court date for Walker v. Kimberlin was approaching, and that this escalation of harassment was not merely coincidental. It's just like Rauhauser, in his "Carlito2000" persona, trying to get Barrett Brown to go after me and Patterico. If Barrett didn't realize he was being manipulated, I sure as hell did and, to repeat: Homey don't play that game. *And there you are, once again, formulating opinions based on a faulty hypothesis. Get the hypothesis correct. THEN form opinions.*

Your Non-Coincidental Curiosity

That's something else you perhaps ought to think about, Mr. Schmalfeldt: Neal Rauhauser is much smarter than you are. *(Never met him, spoke to him once. Seems like a nice guy in a quirky way.)* Perhaps less crazy, but definitely much smarter. Barrett Brown has never figured that out, and maybe he never will, but the one thing I've never done is to underestimate Neal Rauhauser's evil cunning. *I am not Barrett Brown.*

People who once worked with Rauhauser have used words like "scary" and "dangerous" to describe him. *I've never "worked" with Rauhauser.* Also, "impulsive" — his great weakness: Neal is prone to cook up a scheme and act on it without considering what would seem to be predictable second- and third-degree consequences. Yet Neal is exceptionally intelligent (one former friend estimated Neal's IQ at 160), and remarkably adept at identifying the kind of people he can dishonestly manipulate for his own evil purposes. Neal took advantage of Barrett Brown's susceptibility, inspiring Barrett to contact both me and Patterico, apparently in an effort to get . . .

Well, I have a good hunch what Neal's purpose was, but let's not go into that, eh? *(Your hunches are not evidence anyway.)* The point is that Neal used Barrett, and Barrett's mental state was such that he didn't seem to understand he was being used, and next thing you know, there's Barrett on YouTube screaming like a lunaticabout how he's going to "destroy" an FBI agent. Oops.

Tough luck there, Barrett. But I digress . . . *(God, how you ramble.)*

Your interest in my whereabouts, and my wife's employment, and my income as a journalist — your curiosity about me is apparently not just coincidental, is it, Mr. Schmalfeldt? *(No. Not at all. It's based on MY wanting to know if and why your are lying about your "relocation," knowing that no reputable news organization will hire you with your history of race-baiting and overt racism and misogyny, and your — in my opinion — dishonest panhandling. Odd as it may seem, I have my own mind. I think my own thoughts. I come up with my own questions without help from Rauhauser, Kimberlin, Santa Claus or the Easter Bunny.)*

Even if you're merely crazy *(again with the incorrect preconceived notion and unscientific analysis of my intent and behavior)* and not employed or sponsored by Brett Kimberlin *(as I have said time and time again I am not)*, it is not by random chance that you became obsessed with me, and I have always viewed your threats and demands and other forms of harassment in the context of a larger story. *("Obsessed" is not a word I would use as far as my thoughts about you, but about your thoughts regarding me. But again, you have formulated an opinion based on a faulty hypothesis, decided your faulty assumption is TRUTH, and are operating as if it were engraved in a stone tablet.)* But you have no right to know anything about me or my family, and I have no obligation to answer any of your questions, or to take notice of your malicious accusations. *(I claim the same right YOU claim — that of a journalist.)*

Your obvious motive — to assist Brett Kimberlin in silencing Kimberlin's critics — *(and again, the faulty assumption based on the incorrect hypothesis and declared as truth)* is sufficient cause for me to dismiss you as an active agent of evil. *(Oh, please.)* Having never e-mailed you before, I checked my inbox and found that you had e-mailed me three times: *(Oh! The HARASSMENT!)*

From Bill Schmalfeldt (balmerliberal@comcast.net)
Tue Aug 28 11:31:15 2012
To: r.s.mccain@att.net
Subject: One more thing…
I notice I am forbidden from commenting on your blog.
You are not forbidden to comment on mine. Why am I
forbidden to comment on yours? Different opinions not

welcome?
Just wondering.
Bill

Notice the date there? Aug. 28 — nearly a week before your name ever appeared on my blog, you e-mailed to ask why you were banned from commenting at my blog. *(One has nothing to do with the other. I knew of you as I was digging into the National Bloggers Club story, was reading you on a regular basis, and could not understand why someone so "dedicated" to the pursuit of "truth" would delete opposing viewpoints.)*

But you had already been banned from Daily Kos and banned from Examiner.com, so why were commenting privileges at my blog of such interest to you, Mr. Schmalfeldt? *(Again, you lie about the Examiner. Why do you do that? Where is your proof that I was "banned" from the Examiner? I QUIT the Examiner because they wanted to do background checks on all their writers, and I felt that to be an unnecessary invasion of privacy for a $300-month gig. Why do you insist on perpetuating that lie?)* Look up "troll rights" — *(again, the faulty hypothesis used to establish a certified truth. YOU call me a troll, therefore I AM a troll and that is the end of the discussion.)* this insane idea that you and other trolls have, that other people are under some kind of obligation to provide their bandwidth to you so that you can spew you hatefulness *(I do not hate you or anyone else. In fact, I pray to God every night to keep hate from creeping into my heart, lest I end up like you)* to their readers. In other words, not content to befoul your own corner of the Internet (where no sane person would ever go), *(again, an opinion* *based on a faulty hypothesis declared as truth)* you demand that other people provide you access to their platform, so you can befoul that, too. *I demand nothing, Mr. McCain. I ask. If you decline, I can demand until I'm blue in the face (or ashen grey, like you) and it will do no good.*

Do I really have to explain what "fuck you" means, Bill? *(No. It defines your limited ability to express yourself.)*

OK, second e-mail*: (Sigh.)*

From Bill Schmalfeldt (bill@patriot-ombudsman.com)
Wed Nov 21 08:18:12 2012
To: r.s.mccain@att.net
Did you and Louann ever REALLY move, or is that just part of the scam?
#WAR
Bill Schmalfeldt
Editor
The Patriot-Ombudsman

To this, sir, you attached a satellite photo map and a "background report" about my former address in Maryland. There were errors in that report — e.g., "10 baths"? – and it's been years since either of those phone numbers were mine or my wife's. However, the address was correct for the home we moved out of last year, for reasons that are well-known (there are many witnesses), but which you and Brett Kimberlin and Neal Rauhauser keep constantly lying about. But why get into that, eh? *(I am not a liar, sir. I am also not a pedophile. But more about that later.)*

The point is, we moved, and on Nov. 21, you sent me this e-mail, accusing me of a "scam." Shortly thereafter, you began harassing me non-stop on Twitter, using your "Liberal Grouch" account which, if I recall correctly, was subsequently deleted because of your repeated terms-of-service violations. (Maybe you could refresh my memory about this, Bill — you've been banned so many places, it's hard to keep track.) *No, you are incorrect. I still hold "Liberal Grouch" in abeyance so scumbags like you can't use it like you have used other Twitter accounts I have abandoned. And I have been banned from ONE website. And not for the reasons you and your fellow idiots keep harping on.*

And finally the third e-mail: *(Good lord....)*
From: Bill Schmalfeldt (grouchcast@comcast.net)
Thu Dec 20 11:22:15 2012
To: r.s.mccain@att.net
Subject: Hi, Pal!
I do a BlogTalk Radio Show now. It's on Weekdays, live from noon to 1pm. You seem like a nervy guy. Wanna be my guest? I'll play nice if you do.
Love to have you!
Bill Schmalfeldt

Well, har-dee-har-har, "chum." And did you notice anything unusual about your e-mails to me, Bill? Three e-mails, three addresses: In August, you e-mailed me from balmerliberal@comcast.net. In November, you e-mailed me from bill@patriot-ombudsman.com. And then in December, you e-mailed me from grouchcast@comcast.net. *(The two comcast addresses are on the same account. The first, "balmerliberal" was created so that people writing to me about articles I wrote as "The Baltimore Liberal Examiner" on Examiner.com would not be mixed into my regular e-mail. When I created the Patriot-Ombudsman website, I created the Patriot-Ombudsman e-mail for the same reason, to keep that e-mail separate from my regular account. The "grouchcast" e-mail is part of my main Comcast account (you get, I think, something like 10 separate account with Comcast) so I could keep the GROUCHCAST SHOW e-mail separated from other accounts. Nothing nefarious, easily explained. Except, it would seem, to a fool.)* Three separate e-mail accounts you used in less than four months, which probably doesn't seem that strange to you, because you have used so many online identities in the past year or two: "Liberal Grouch," "Dead Breitbart," "Patriot Ombudsman," "Bill Matthews" and so forth. But while this may seem normal to you, regular people tend to look at that kind of multiple-personality behavior and think: CRAZY. *(Especially if they are operating on a faulty hypothesis and using it to formulate opinions that have no basis in truth.)*

There is also the apparent instability of your mood, the way you address someone as "chum" and then accuse them of a "scam" while sending a map of (what you think is) their home, in other words: "I know where you live!" And then a few weeks later, this false-friendly invitation — "Love to have you!" — sent to someone you spent months doing everything in your power to harm. *Oh, now, really Mr. McCain. How have I ever attempted to "harm" you? Sakes!*

This is not how sane, decent and honest people behave, Mr. Schmalfeldt, *(because you, the eminent psychologist, racist and drunk say so?)* and yet you can't seem to help yourself. You are apparently in the throes of some sort of compulsion that causes you to constantly harass and threaten people. *(Again, the faulty hypothesis comes into play, coloring your perceptions of reality. You might consider getting yourself checked. Dry out first.)* In complaining that I had violated your copyright, you provided a list of posts, but I could write every day about your craziness if I thought anyone wanted to read it.

The list is a list of posts where you use images that do not belong to you. They are mine, and I have not given you permission to use them. It is really quite that simple.

There's no shortage of craziness on your part for me to write about, but I ignore most of it, because it has become so tedious: "Oh, look – Bill did something crazy again today." *(Again, the faulty hypothesis, but I do grow weary of pointing that out to you.)* And of course, you'll do something crazy tomorrow, and the day after that. Basically, if it's a day of the week ending in "-y," Bill Schmalfeldt is doing something crazy. Dog bites man.

Day after day, you cyberstalk and harass people, *(what YOU call "journalism" when YOU do it)* and it's just like what I said about Barrett Brown:

(Snip. I am not Barrett Brown. Irrelevant.)

The Dragon Kicks Sir William's Ass

You begin with the assumption that everyone else is your inferior. *(Well, YOU are. But everyone else? There's that faulty hypothesis again.)* Then you set out with the intention of demonstrating this — and imagining how you'll be admired by others for displaying your superiority *(Egad! It now claims MIND READING abilities!)* — by bullying someone you consider your inferior, and when this expedition does not produce the expected result, you believe you have been wronged. *(Again, the faulty hypothesis.)*

Your rationalization of your failure *(TFH is how we'll abbreviate "the faulty hypothesis" hereonin.)* is essentially this: "Those inferior people somehow cheated me out of my glory. It's unfair that, because of their deceit and malice, my superiority has been wrongfully obscured and I have been deprived of my right to admiration." *TFH and mind reading.*

So you sally forth from the castle, the knight in shining armor who is going to slay the dragon, and after the dragon kicks your ass, you limp back to the castle complaining that the dragon didn't play fair. *(TFH)* You are a victim of your own irrational expectations, *(Mindreading and TFH)* your arrogant overestimation of your abilities *(TFH and mindreading)*, and your contempt for your chosen enemies *(TFH and Mindreading.)*. Whose fault is it, Mr. Schmalfeldt, that Aaron Walker, Lee Stranahan and John Hoge have refused to tolerate your bullying ways? *(TFH about "bullying" when you do it you call it "journalism.)* Why did you think they were under any obligation to conform to your will? *(They were not under any obligation. I never said they were under any obligation. And when did I ever demand that anyone "conform to my will"? TFH.)* And why, if you are going to behave in this manner, do you object to my describing your actions — and illustrating those descriptions with photos of you? *(Because you are using photos you have no right to use. I own them. I hold the copyright. You did not ask permission. Therefore, you are not allowed to use them.)*

Your problem is not my writing about you. Your problem is you. (Gee, Dr. Freud.)

Let's talk photos, just briefly.

(Snip. I am not Amanda Bynes. She is a celebrity. I am not. Using her photo to illustrate a news event qualifies for fair use. Use of a person's image, dishonestly cropped to make him appear malicious, is not. My uploading a photo or a movie to the Internet does not give you the right to use it. In fact, each photo and movie comes with the explicit notice, "Copyright Bill Schmalfeldt, ALL RIGHTS RESERVED. You never ASKED to use them, you just used them. I am not Ed Shultz. He is a celebrity. He has a TV and radio show. His image is covered by fair use. You can not just take the image of a private citizen, manipulate it to your purposes, and use it. It is the same thing as coming into my house, taking a commemorative dish with a picture of my late mother on it, saying the image was already online, and walking away with it. This will not stand the "fair use" sniff test.")

Perhaps I am completely misunderstanding this stuff, and the Legal Department will tell me I'm all wrong. Maybe the case of Schmalfeldt v. McCain will be a legal landmark by which all bloggers are put on notice to stop all this YouTube screen-capping and grabbing photos off social-media accounts under penalty of brutal compensatory damages awarded to a notorious kook in a Maryland trailer park. You are far down on the list, McCain. First, there are the 23 instances of perjury in Mr. Akbar's letter to Zippy Kid.

The court will award you umpteen gazillion dollars, Bill, because of the way in which I shamelessly "stole" your photos, and this verdict will stand as a warning to any other right-wing blogger who thinks he can get away with saying mean things about Bill Schmalfeldt on the Internet. Yes, imagine the headlines:
Schmalfeldt Triumphs; Supreme Court Ruling
Reverses Years of Online Injustice

(Grow up, for fuck's sake.)
Oh, damn! I guess I'm just being sarcastic again. Lost my train of thought and forgot that I started this e-mail with the intent of explaining something very important: YOU'RE CRAZY.
And also, fuck you.
Sincerely,
Robert Stacy McCain
Whereabouts Unknown *(Isn't that where all the masked wrestlers come from?)*

Backatcha, buddy.

Chapter 7 – THE LEAGUE OF LICKSPITTLES

Hoge and his friends have done a fine job on me.

Law Enforcement has been no help whatsoever. I have presented what I believe to be a rock solid case for harassment under state law 3-803 and 3-805. I have tried to get my home county, Howard County, Maryland, to protect me from this harassment. They shrug their shoulders. If Hoge comes to my house and beats me up, they can do something. But until then? Meh.

I've asked Hoge's home county, Carroll County, Maryland, where he filed all but one of the 367 frivolous, unfounded misdemeanor charges against me over the past 15 months. I've asked them to investigate, to take a look, to see if there is a case for harassment. No reply.

And the harassment continues. And my symptoms continue to worsen.

Before the testicle kick represented by having "Intentional Infliction" pulled from the shelves by Hoge's underhanded "acquisition" of "Paul Krendler's" blog rights, I was able to walk short distances in the house without my roller walker. The next morning, I woke up and am now unable to walk without hanging on to something.

If I let go, I fall.

My chest muscles are getting tighter. It's harder to draw a full breath.

My eyes have difficulty remaining focused. I have to

concentrate to keep them from drifting out of focus.

And they're not done with me yet.

No "Leader" like Hoge would be able to do the damage he's done without the assistance of a loyal cadre of lickspittle lackeys.

These are the ones I've identified so far.

KYLE KIERNAN

An intelligent lad. Writes well. Makes one wonder why he chose a life of crime. He seems to be on a better path these days, but he is still one of Hoge's more effective attack weasels.

LIBRARYGRYFFON

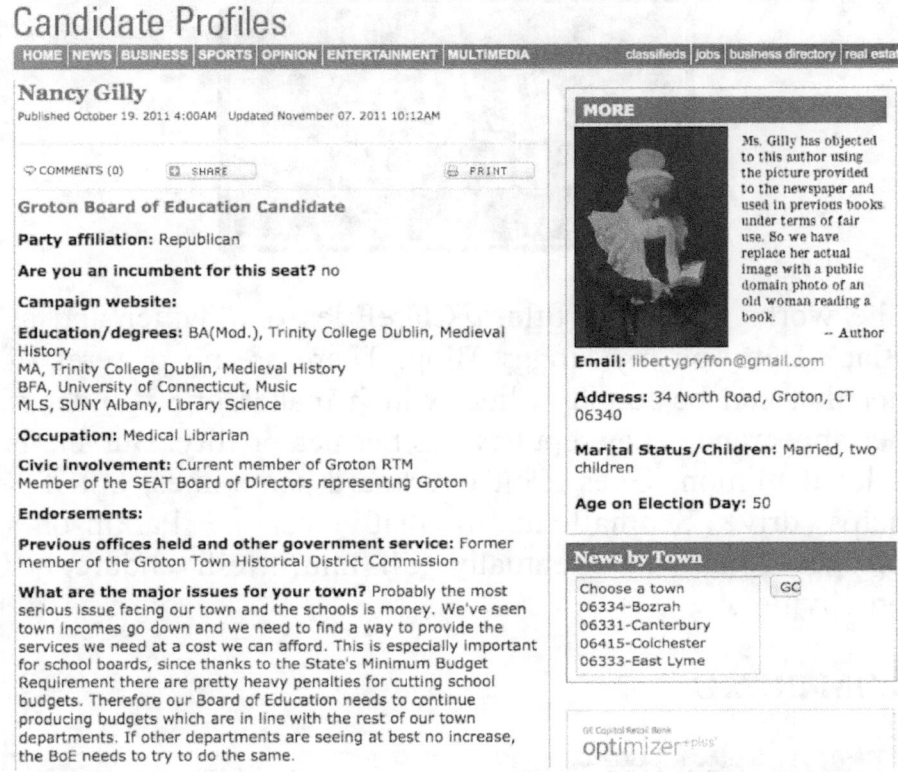

Candidate Profiles

Nancy Gilly

Published October 19. 2011 4:00AM Updated November 07. 2011 10:12AM

💬 COMMENTS (0)   🔗 SHARE   🖨 PRINT

Groton Board of Education Candidate

Party affiliation: Republican

Are you an incumbent for this seat? no

Campaign website:

Education/degrees: BA(Mod.), Trinity College Dublin, Medieval History
MA, Trinity College Dublin, Medieval History
BFA, University of Connecticut, Music
MLS, SUNY Albany, Library Science

Occupation: Medical Librarian

Civic involvement: Current member of Groton RTM
Member of the SEAT Board of Directors representing Groton

Endorsements:

Previous offices held and other government service: Former member of the Groton Town Historical District Commission

What are the major issues for your town? Probably the most serious issue facing our town and the schools is money. We've seen town incomes go down and we need to find a way to provide the services we need at a cost we can afford. This is especially important for school boards, since thanks to the State's Minimum Budget Requirement there are pretty heavy penalties for cutting school budgets. Therefore our Board of Education needs to continue producing budgets which are in line with the rest of our town departments. If other departments are seeing at best no increase, the BoE needs to try to do the same.

MORE

Ms. Gilly has objected to this author using the picture provided to the newspaper and used in previous books under terms of fair use. So we have replace her actual image with a public domain photo of an old woman reading a book.
 -- Author

Email: libertygryffon@gmail.com

Address: 34 North Road, Groton, CT 06340

Marital Status/Children: Married, two children

Age on Election Day: 50

News by Town

Choose a town   GC
06334-Bozrah
06331-Canterbury
06415-Colchester
06333-East Lyme

GE Capital Retail Bank
optimizer⁺ᵖˡᵘˢ

Don't hate her for coming in next to dead last in this election. She claims Aspberger's runs in her family.

Her real name was revealed to be Nancy Gilly. She is also identified as "Pip Van Houten" on the negative reviews written on the previous books Schmalfeldt tried on Amazon. What she lacks in smarts, she makes up for in sheer obsession and dedication.

BETTINA HAPER

She works under the title @ClareFries on Twitter and as Black Betty on my Hoggy Blog. There are no pictures of her that can be found online, which makes one wonder if her appearance is as repulsive as her personality. But she is a loyal minion. Goes a bit overboard sometimes, but if it helps drive Schmalfeldt to that level of Parkinson's madness that will eventually kill him, we'll endure her proclivities.

TOM PUZIO

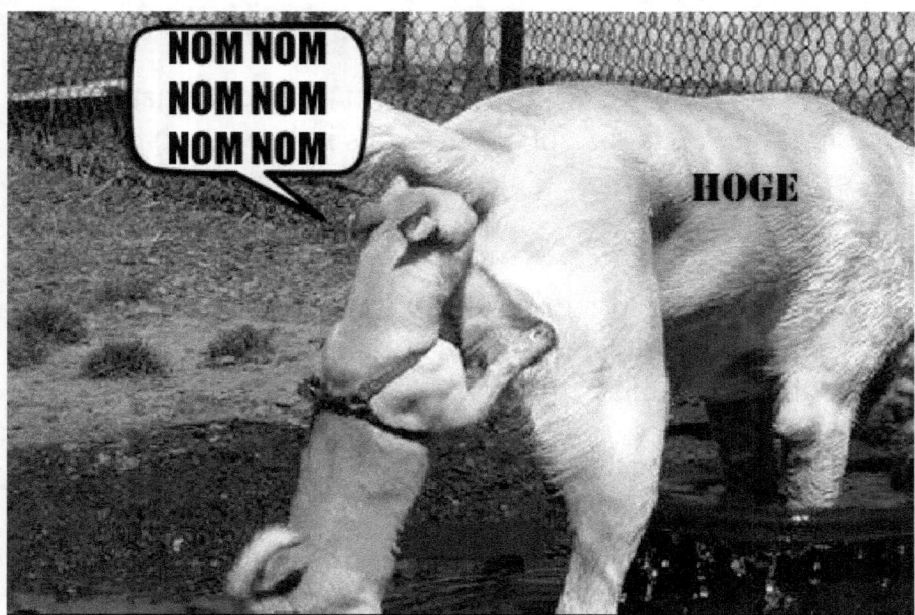

Goes by several names. He was "Tomblvd." Now, he's "Perfect Tommy" or some other such nonsense. He's still "Tomblvd" on Twitter. Drop by and compliment his lovely artwork. The tattoo. As Charles Emerson Winchester said on "M*A*S*H", "the poor man's investment in art."

CHRIS HEATHER

We probably shouldn't give this slacker any recognition as he has been AWOL since Schmalfeldt revealed his identity as a bottom-feeding scum sucker, a former member of the "Occupy Burn Notice" gang that sold him out and revealed his identity. Lovely fellow, but a bit on the cowardly side.

PATRICK G. GRADY

Springtime 4 Pundit @PalatinePundit · 4h
@LibraryGryffon Mr. Bill says, "OOOOOOOOOOOOOOOOOOOOOOH
NOOOOOOOOOOOOOOOOOOO! @ParkyBillTweets
pic.twitter.com/dHcaTW3gKY
↶ Reply ⇄ Retweet ★ Favorite   Flag media

Operates under the name @PalatinePundit. Works at an Office Max in Palatine, IL. He is admittedly bipolar and says his wife won't let him achieve his real dreams. Clever lad, he Tweeted this picture to Schmalfeldt

ROBIN CAUSEY

I am not a perfect human being. I do make mistakes. When investigating a person, I rely on that person to give me honest answers to the questions I ask.

Robin Causey preferred to play "Cutsey Pie" to impress his conservative readers on his former "Evilconservatives.net" website. I thought I had compiled enough evidence to claim that Causey was the individual operating on Twitter as "Embryriddlealum." I was incorrect.

But Causey is not without guilt.

Believing Causey to be Embryriddlealum and knowing that person was using a picture of my dead mother as a Twitter avatar, I called Causey and demanded he remove the picture. He hung up on me. I tried calling back, but he just let the phone ring.

My sister believed that perhaps she could reason with his wife, MaryFrances Causey, a prominent member of the college community in Yavapai County, Arizona, by appealing to her sense as a mother about the wrongness of someone posting disfigured photo of our dead mother as a method to attack me.

Mr. and Mrs. Causey responded by filing a Injunction Against Harassment against me. So much for the motherly instinct thing. I have no problem not contacting the Causeys, except for the fact that they lied under oath on their forms, saying that I had been previously arrested for "domestic abuse." Never happened.

Causey and I have a long history.

From an article I published on January 12, 2012.

http://www.beyondprose.com/index.php/testimonies-facebook-experiences-58133/

It was late November 2011. I was an independent contractor reporter for the mega local news agency known as the Examiner. I had just put the wraps on an investigative piece about a Georgia militia leader taking over a subdivision in northwest Georgia and using it as his private militia training ground, when I got a tip about some alleged nefarious activities going on in Wisconsin.

Seems as if a gang of Facebook bullies was trying to throw a wrench into the effort to collect petitions to recall Wisconsin governor Scott Walker. This gang, calling itself "Operation Burn Notice" seemed to center around one individual calling himself "Operation Burn Notice". This gang was an offshoot of another Facebook gang of thugs called "Knot My Wisconsin" - a group of trolls bounced from the legitimate pro-recall "Not in My Wisconsin" Facebook page. As sort of a "flashing the gang colors" thing, the banished trolls generally use the word "knot" instead of "not" in their Facebook postings. Many of the same players were involved in the Operation Burn Notice gang.

The purpose of the Facebook page: to entice people into gathering petitions in the recall effort and then destroy them instead of turning them in. This effort went so far as the creation a phony website - a detail for detail match for the Occupy Madison legitimate site, giving it the URL of "occupy-madison.net" where the actual site was "occupy-madison.org." People who typed ".com" or ".net" instead of ".org" were whisked away to the phony site, where they were told that all the necessary signatures had been gathered and they should not bother to turn in the ones they already had.

In the meantime, my investigation into the "Operation Burn Notice" side of the scam led me to an individual calling himself "Aaron Burr", who operated a website called EvilConservatives.net from his home in Chino Valley, Ariz.

I contacted "Burr" through his e-mail address, "superaaronburr@gmail.com" and we had a spirited e-conversation in which he revealed he was just having some fun with the nitwits in Wisconsin, that he was just a "hired gun" paid by "some guy who liked my writing" and he would reveal the identity of his benefactor if the price was right.

All of this made national website news when the progressive "AlterNet" site published a story in December, called "Bullies, Liars and Impostors: How Facebook and Go Daddy Shield Scott Walker's Online Guerillas".

While this story was generating controversy, I began a series on the Examiner about some of the individual members who were not hiding behind false names and sock puppets. That's when I was fired from the Examiner.

Too Close to the Truth?

One of the Wisconsin participants in "Operation Burn Notice" contacted the Denver headquarters of Examiner.com, a company owned by ultra-conservative billionaire Philip Anschutz - an individual who had made personal donations to the tune of $10,000 to Gov. Walker since the beginning of 2011. This individual told the Examiner legal department that I had been publishing stories that were defamatory without checking facts. Nobody from the Examiner bothered to check the stories. Nobody could be troubled to contact me to get my side of the argument. I was told my services were no longer required and all my stories were wiped from the Examiner servers.

I probably would have moved on to other territories, but the "Operation Burn Notice" gang was not satisfied with getting me fired. Now they wanted to mock me. They stole copyrighted images from my personal website (which had a copyright notice in a big blue box on the front page and every other page, altered them, posted them on their Facebook page, and then filled up the page with comments... mostly having to do with the size of my genitalia (?) and the fact that I have Parkinson's disease. My personal favorite was the one that showed my head being "extruded" from the back end of a turtle.

Although the Parkinson's disease insults not only offend me, but they are a shot at the 1.5 million of us in America who have this debilitating neurological disorder.

First, I filed a Copyright and DMCA complaint with Facebook claiming ownership of the images. Then, someone identifying himself as William Jenkins filed a counter claim, stating that I did not own the images and was just harassing the Facebook group. The thing about these Facebook claims? When you "electronically" sign them, you are agreeing that what you are saying is the truth, "under penalty of perjury."

Let's focus on William Jenkins for a moment. Earlier investigations proved that the occupation he listed on his Facebook profile, "Union Slave for the Kenosha Unified School District", were not true. The media spokesperson for the KUSD answered my e-mail query stating that there is not now nor has there ever been a William Jenkins working for the district.

When you fill out one of these Facebook claims, you reveal your name, address, phone number and e-mail address. Jenkins address turned out to be the post office box of a failed electronics company in Antioch, Ill. The phone number he gave was that of a nice, church-going Kenosha couple who told me they had never heard of William Jenkins. The e-mail address, "williejenkins666@gmail.com"... well, do a Google search on your own to see the sort of vile filth he posts using that address.I contacted Facebook about Jenkins, how he had given either a false name, a false address and definitely a false phone number "under penalty of perjury." I wrote about this on my Facebook page. And when I arose from my slumber the next morning...

I had no Facebook account. It had been disabled. Deleted. Enough of the sock puppet personas and real people at Operation Burn Notice were seemingly upset by the truth being told, and spammed Facebook with complaints about how my Facebook post about outing Jenkins' falsehoods were a "violation of community standards."

Fired from the Examiner. No more Facebook.

All because I followed a story where it led.

I began to backtrace. I looked at the AlterNet story again and decided to see if I could make a definitive connection between the phony Occupy-Madison page (which had been outed by the AlterNet story and was now just publishing anti-Occupy Wall Street propaganda) and the gang at Operation Burn Notice. And while I could not find a direct link between the two organizations, I did discover that the phony Occupy-Madison page was using photo stock from Getty Images. They prefer to be paid for their images instead of having them picked like fruit from low hanging branches. I notified the legal department at Getty, then notified the webmaster at the phony Occupy site, which folded faster than Superman on laundry day. (The image of the couple kissing on their header, for instance, was taken by Getty Images at the Vancouver Soccer riots. Getty informed me that the webmaster of the phony site faced charges of anywhere from $490 to $2000 for each unauthorized use of their photos. And there were a lot of

Getty Images on the site.) Now, there's a standard "GoDaddy" parked domain page on the site. But my investigation into the site led to an idea I hoped would have deeper ramifications.

Follow the Money

The phony Occupy site had a donation button on it. For some reason, instead of directing the button to themselves, they picked a legitimate 501(c)(3) charity called Occupy, Inc., operated by a pastor in Edmond, Okla. (The pastor says he was in no way connected with the scam and never saw a penny from the phony site.) But before coming to that realization, I recalled that "Aaron Burr" had told me he was just a "hired gun" being paid to "stir up trouble" in Wisconsin. He even bragged about it on his Evil Conservatives site, saying he was making a few bucks on all the trouble he was causing, and that he "owned" the state of Wisconsin. I wondered if the guy whose name was listed on the charity the donation on the phony Occupy site might not be the guy who was the money behind "Burr's" efforts.

I wrote again to "Burr's" e-mail. No response. So, I checked the WHOIS information on the Evil Conservatives site and found Burr's name, address, phone number and other information. Using the web-tracking service Spokeo, I tracked down the information. It led... not to an Aaron Burr, but to a Robin Wesley Causey of Chino Valley, Ariz. In one of my communications with "Burr" he mentioned having a PO Box in Chino Valley. Chino Valley is 17 miles from Prescott, Ariz., where self-professed "rich boy" Operation Burn Notice member "Howard Earl" says he studied at Embry-Riddle Aeronautical University.

Having regained access to Facebook, I decided it was time to fight fire with fire. I created a page which identifies Aaron Burr as Robin Wesley Causey, formerly of Larkspur, Calif., now of Chino Valley, Ariz.

I can generally tell how close I am to my mark when things start disappearing from the Internet. This morning, Jan. 11, 2012, my Facebook page regarding Causey has been removed from the service. All references to Causey have been deleted from Operation Burn Notice's new Facebook presence as well as from Knot My Wisconsin's Facebook pages. "Howard Earl" states on his Facebook profile that he studied at Embry-Riddle Aeronautical University in Prescott, Ariz. The legal department at ERAU says nobody by that name ever graduated from that university. They don't seem to care much for someone misidentifying himself as an alumnus, especially given the things "Howard" has written on his various Facebook pages, so "Howard" can expect to be contacted to "explain himself".

When "Operation Burn Notice" petered out, Causey went back to his other pursuits, which seem to be that of a house husband for a woman who is active in the Chino Valley, Arizona, educational scene.

Another former Operation Burn Notice member, however, needed to keep the war going for some reason.

CHRIS HEATHER

From my Patriot-Ombudsman blog, dated April 28, 2014.

Ah, yes. **@Embryriddlealum.** The twitter scum who keeps telling me to "Take The Cure."

Operation Burn Notice
This hour is brought to you by the CURE FOR PARKINSON'S DISEASE.

Like · Comment · Share · Sunday at 2:54pm ·

5 people like this.

Oh, that's back when he called himself "Operation Burn Noti

Let me share with you just how I came to finally identify Heather as "Embryriddlealum".

I started to suspect I was wrong about Causey being ERA over the past several days. Even though he is a conservative scumbag and was involved in the Operation Burn Notice nonsense, I contacted one of the senior folks of the former Knot My Wisconsin group with whom I've developed a friendly relationship. He said he was aware of "Aaron Burr" who tweets as "SuperAaronBurr" and is, in fact, Robin Wesley Causey of Chino Valley, AZ. My new friend could not say for sure, but he was fairly certain that Heather was ERA.

So, I laid a little trapsy wapsy for ERA today. I did a search on the Wisconsin Judiciary Case Search and came up with a domestic violence case involving Chris Heather and a girl named Stacy Thomas. I've been taunting ERA with that all afternoon. He gave himself away when I said I had called her and she said the fight was because she made fun of his junk.

ERA, as idiots will do, gave himself away.

Howard Hanger-Earl @embryriddlealum · 58m
@wmsbroadcasting So you can talk to corpses now, Shake? You poor dumb bastard. You should come with a tuning key I play you so often...

Expand   ↰ Reply   ⇄ Retweet   ★ Favorite   ••• More

Hah. So, he knows Stacy Thomas had shuffled off the mortal coil. Keep in mind, I did not mention Chris Heather at all in my taunting of ERA today. In fact, I covered his name on the Wisconsin repo

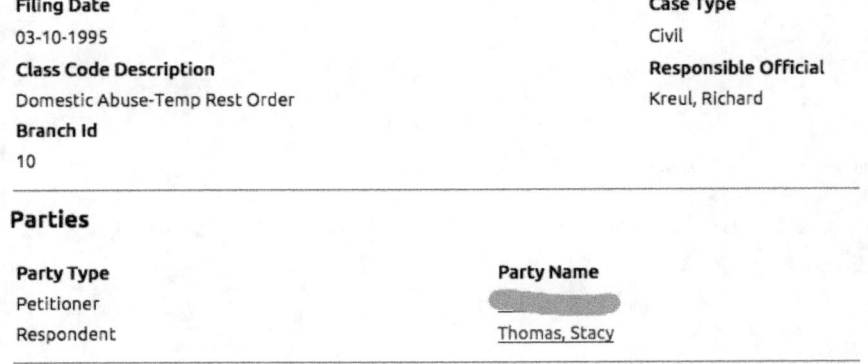

Filing Date	Case Type
03-10-1995	Civil
Class Code Description	**Responsible Official**
Domestic Abuse-Temp Rest Order	Kreul, Richard
Branch Id	
10	

Parties

Party Type	Party Name
Petitioner	████████████
Respondent	Thomas, Stacy

Like a big old catfish, Heather, or ERA if you will, took the bait. The rest was just legwork... so to speak.

1. ERA knows a Stacy Thomas and knows she is dead.

2. Stacy Thomas was the respondent in a domestic abuse case, which means she beat Chris Heather up. Here's the original file.

Chris Heather vs Stacy Thomas

Racine County Case Number 1995CV000128

Filing Date
03-10-1995

Case Type
Civil

Class Code Description
Domestic Abuse-Temp Rest Order

Responsible Official
Kreul, Richard

Branch Id
10

Parties

Party Type	Party Name
Petitioner	Heather, Chris
Respondent	Thomas, Stacy

Now this all happened in 1995. We know that Chris Heather lives in Racine.

The information contained in this report was compiled from thousands of local and national data public records databases to deliver the most comprehensive, accurate and up-to-date information available.

Name

Chris Heather

Age	Date of Birth	Phone Number
40	8/1973	262-639-9437

Additional Phone Numbers

262-639-2891

Most Recent Address

2830 Arlington Ave, Uppr, Racine, WI 53403-4208

So, where did Stacy Thomas live in 1995?

Contact Report
Stacy Thomas

Name	Stacy Thomas
Age	Died in 2010 (35)
Date of Birth	2/26/1975
Phone Number	276-632-9430
Additional Phone Numbers	262-898-9999, 262-637-7092, 262-639-2889
Most Recent Address	2385 Stillmeadow Rd, Axton, VA 24054-3325
Aliases/Name Variations	Stacy L Thomas, Stacey L Thomas, S Thomas, Thomas Stacy

Email:

t****@yxxxx.cxx	**Stacy Thomas** 2385 Stillmeadow Rd Axton, VA 24054
k****@aol.com	**Stacy Thomas** 2385 Stillmeadow Rd Axton, VA 24054-3325
l****@juno.com	**Stacy Thomas** 2385 Stillmeadow Rd Axton, VA 24054-3325
s****@msn.com	**Stacy Thomas** 1316 Askin St Martinsville, VA 24112-4602

13 addresses were found

Address	City, State, Zip	Phone	Added	Updated
2385 Stillmeadow Rd	Axton, VA 24054-3325		1/2009	1/2009
1316 Askin St	Martinsville, VA 24112-4602	276-632-9430	3/2008	6/2008
2040 Quincy Ave, Apt 1	Racine, WI 53403-4233	262-898-9999	12/2005	12/2005
3116 Washington Ave	Racine, WI 53405-3050	xxx-639-2889	3/1998	3/1998
4122 Sheridan Rd	Mount Pleasant, WI 53403-3817		3/1995	3/1995
3155 Coolidge Ave	Mount Pleasant, WI 53403-3511		6/1993	6/1993

And you will notice she died in 2010. In Virginia.

According to the Social Security Death Index....

Stacy L Thomas, "United States Social Security Death Index"

Given Name:	Stacy
Middle Name:	L
Surname:	Thomas
Name Suffix:	
Birth Date:	26 February 1975
Social Security Number:	398-82-4968
State:	Wisconsin
Last Place of Residence:	Martinsville, Henry, Virginia
Previous Residence Postal Code:	24112
Event Date:	11 April 2010
Age:	35

So...

A. Chris Heather got beat up by Stacy Thomas

B. I disguised Heather's name on the court report and accused ERA of getting beaten up by a girl.

C. ERA denied it all.

D. I told him I talked to her and she made fun of his penis size.

E. ERA says, "Oh, you can talk to corpses?" Meaning he knows she's dead.

F. A simple search finds Stacy L. Thomas, who once lived 5 miles away from Chris Heather, died in Virginia in 2010. She's the right age, or... was, I should say.

G. I never once mentioned the name "Chris Heather" in my taunt.

Therefore:

A+B+C+D+E+F+G=ERA is CHRIS HEATHER!

From Lisa Weed's Facebook Page, Lisa with Chris Heather.

Chapter 8 – AND ON IT GOES

I have no expectation that any of this is going to make a difference. But at least there will be a record of my side of the story.

Law enforcement isn't interested. I've contacted every member of the state legislature that represents my county and asked them about the possibility of extending cyber bullying protection they give to teenagers to disabled adults who don't have the money to hire a lawyer to ensure that people like Hoge are stopped from this sort of permanently damaging activity.

The Lickspittles love to go on about "all my victims."

What they are upset about is that I would not take "no" for an answer in pursuit of a story.

They are upset that I questioned the fact that Lee Stranahan told three different stories about the stillbirth of his child. Given Stranny's track record of lying and grifting, it seemed like a natural question that could have been answered quite easily.

I "tormented" Stranny by asking the Texas Department of Family and Protective Services to take a check on the Stranahan children to ensure Daddy wasn't using them as punching bags or porno props. Thank God, they were not. But the Lickspittles believe that if the person you have strong suspicions about is a conservative, then it's none of your business and you should just turn away when you suspect children may be abused. That's not even moral, let alone good advice.

I "tormented" Stranny by asking the Dallas Police to look into whether or not some of the near-pubescent girls Stranny photographed in his porno days were of age. Some of them looked like 13-14 year old girls. But Stranny is a conservative, so if you think he might be doing kiddie porn, don't say a word about it.

I "tormented" Stranny by proving that he used to sell his wife's sexual services as a model to be "posed" with by other men with no clothes on.

These "good, moral people" take the side of my ex-wife, a drug abuser, adulteress, liar, self-destructive poor excuse of a mother. But she sides with Stranny and Hoge, so her transgressions must be overlooked and I am called a "cuckold" for DARING to allow her to cheat on me.

It goes on and on and on.

They attack me? That's fine. I respond? They cry VICTIM!

They use a disfigured photo of my dead mother as a Twitter avatar, that's just okey dokey. Someone (not me) starts a Twitter account about "Hoge's Dead Mother" and uses the photo of Norman Bates' dessicated mom from the movie "Psycho" as an avatar, they rend their garments and cry "BLASPHEMY."

"Beware the Ides of March" is a death threat, because Hoge says so. Any sin that I'm accused of, if committed by a conservative, is immediately absolved. Any lie told, if it casts me in a bad light, is acceptable.

It's OK to lie about the extent of my Parkinson's disease.

Anything they can (and will) do to make my life miserable is fair game.

When I stop responding, they ratchet up the pressure to try to force me into response. If I change my blog URL or Twitter Account, they hunt me down like bloodhounds so they can watch my every move to report to Daddy Hoge.

No, I don't think they're done with me. I believe when this peace order expires in December, Hoge will at least attempt to get another one. I'm sure I'm in for another run of criminal charges. The Lickspittles are already quacking about something bad that is going to happen to me, and soon.

It is May 2, 2014. They haven't killed me. They've destroyed my reputation, but I am not my reputation. My wife loves me, so do my kids, so do my dogs, so does my remaining family.

No, they haven't killed me yet. They'll keep trying.

If they're going to succeed, and if Law Enforcement isn't interested in protecting me, I ask God to call me home soon.

I don't fear death. I fear life under constant harassment,

And, I have decided to fight back

Chapter 9 – THE LAWSUIT

After this book went public, it seems like the readership at Hogewash went nuts. The Grand Hoge itself purchased a copy of the e-book and proclaimed I should have had it reviewed by a competent attorney before publication. That means he can find no reason to kill this one. I am not worried about being sued. First of all, I don't have anything. Second, truth is the ultimate defense to libel. I can prove every word I've written in this book.

Realizing there was nothing they could do to me, they decided to attack the benefactor of this book, the people to whom I plan to donate the profits from the sale of this book.

They attacked the National Parkinson Foundation.

The Hoge reader EWPJ launched the effort by "doxing" one of the officers of the NPF and swarming her with e-mails and phone calls. "How dare they take my dirty money earned from selling books that tell the truth about WJJ Hoge and his minion of right wing haters?"

The meme spread. This is a Sunday night. So I wrote an e-mail to the Sheriff of Carroll County, Maryland (Where Hoge resides), the chief deputy and field operations officer at Carroll County, the Carroll County State's Attorney and his assistant.

For good measure, I threw in the Howard County State's Attorney and his assistant, since that's where I live.

May 4, 2014

Dear Sheriff Tregoning, Col. Kasten and Major Long:

I am writing to you because I am sincerely at a loss as to what to do next. Since February 2013, I have been the victim of systemic harassment and other crimes committed by Mr. William John Joseph Hoge III of 20 Ridge Road, Westminster. I have reported these events to you in the past and have received no reply.

I write with a sense of urgency. Ordinarily, I suppose, the correct thing to do would be to dig into my savings, hire a lawyer, and try to sue Mr. Hoge. For reasons I will outline, that is impossible.

First, please be aware that I am copying the State's Attorneys offices in Carroll and Howard County on this letter. They are very familiar with my complaint, although they have shown no real inclination to do anything about it except to dismiss the 367 criminal charges Mr. Hoge has filed against me in the past year. That is not a misprint. 367 charges, one in Howard County, the rest in Carroll County where Mr. Hoge was somehow able to convince your Court Commissioners that I had committed crimes against him. In June 2013, on his third try, Mr. Hoge was successful in gaining a peace order against me from Carroll County Circuit Court Judge Thomas Stansfield. My "crime" was using the @mention function on Twitter when writing ABOUT Mr. Hoge. His attorney, Zoa Barnes (who I believe, and please correct me if I am incorrect, is the sister-in-law of the Carroll County SA), managed to convince the judge that blocking me on Twitter — an act as easy as pushing a button on the keyboard — would be the same thing as disabling a portion of Mr. Hoge's Internet functionality, and would be akin to having to change his telephone number to avoid telemarketers. Judge Stansfield stated on the stand in June, then again in December when the judge extended the peace order an additional six months, that he had no idea what "the Twitter" was or how to use it. He declared he didn't own a computer or a cellphone. But he ruled, against the decision that Twitter is not to be considered "personal contact" as decided in US v. Cassidy, and as defined by a Maryland Attorney General opinion.

Since receiving his peace order, Mr. Hoge has written hundreds of defamatory blog posts about me that I am not allowed to respond to. He has a couple dozen very dedicated followers who make my life miserable with their constant haranguing. It would be an easy matter to "not read" Mr. Hoge's blog, but the problem does not end there. They troll me on Twitter, they send me anonymous e-mails, and they have just started interfering in my business affairs.

On April 23, I self-published a book on CreateSpace.com called "Intentional Infliction." This book is intended to raise money for the National Parkinson Foundation while raising the question as to why there are no protections for indigent disabled adults against cyber bullying in Maryland. To illustrate the level of harassment I have been forced to endure, I employed the "Fair Use" provisions of the US copyright laws to include a portion of a blog post by the pseudonymous "Paul Krendler". The link to the blog post is below. In this blog post, he libels and defames me. Even worse, he libels and defames my wife.

Warning: This is particularly vile.

http://thinkingmanszombie.wordpress.com/2014/04/23/we-can-write-whatever-we-want-right/

"Krendler" claims he wrote the post in revenge for a blog post I wrote, I don't remember when, but I pulled it down almost immediately because I was ashamed of it.

When my book went public on CreateSpace and Amazon, "Krendler" was approached by Mr. Hoge. Here is the Twitter transaction between the two of them on Apr. 29 — six days after the book was published.

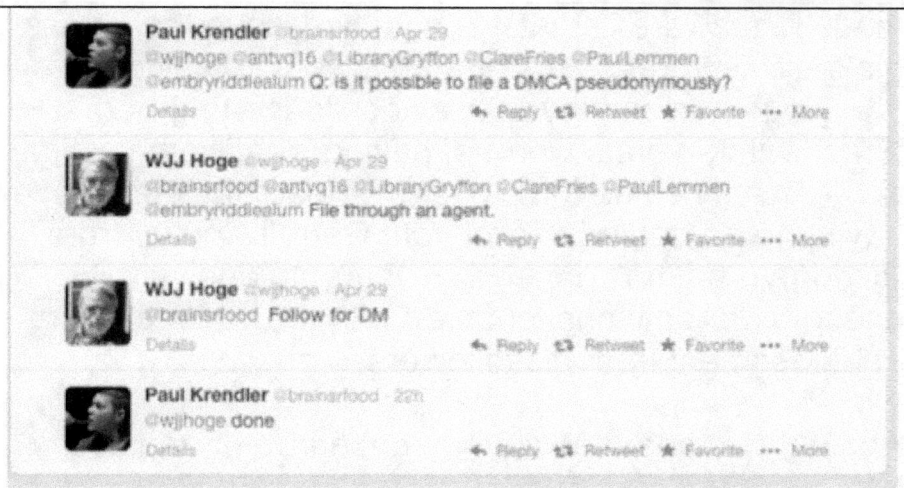

The next day, Mr. Hoge contacted CreateSpace and claimed he owned the rights to the blog post, having "purchased" the "world book and e-book rights" to it.

CreateSpace immediately pulled the book offline and suggested I work out the details with Mr. Hoge, which I cannot do because I am legally forbidden to contact him.

I understand his desire to keep the public from reading this book, since it outlines the details of the past year of harassment. Thousands of blog posts, "tweets" and e-mails, all — in my opinion — with one goal in mind.

Mr. Hoge knows… and knew before he filed his first charge against me in Feb. 2013… that I have been suffering from Parkinson's disease since 2000. I am retired from my GS-13 position with the National Institutes of Health as a result. Mr. Hoge did not give me PD. But he is aware… which I know because I made him aware… that it is a settled issue that stress makes PD progress faster than it would on its own. Mr. Hoge has employed this knowledge to great effect, with a year's worth of having significant jail time and heavy fines hanging over my head, the stress of having to be hauled to and from Carroll County from Elkridge (I haven't driven in 5 years) to answer his peace order petitions, coupled with the various forms of harassment from his followers.

Again, I can hear you saying "get a lawyer and sue him."

My reply, "I don't think I am going to live long enough to see a lawsuit through."

With each new outrage by Hoge, my disease gets worse. A week ago, I could walk short distances in my house without my roller walker. Now, if I let go, I fall. I am having difficulty breathing as my chest muscles are now affected. Typing this e-mail is taking far longer than it should since it is difficult to keep my hands at keyboard level. My eyes go in and out of focus.

Knowing how long it takes to prosecute a lawsuit, I just don't see being able to do it. Besides the fact that I can't find an attorney willing to work on contingency (believe me, I've tried).

I believe I have satisfactorily demonstrated that Mr. Hoge can be brought to trial and be successfully prosecuted for a number of charges.

Harassment under 3-803
Misuse of Electronic Communication under 3-805
Stalking under 3-802
Filing a Fraudulent Lien under 3-808 (his false claim of ownership of "Krendler's" blog)
Fraud under 1-401 (theft by obtaining personal property [the rights to my book] by false pretenses)
Perjury under 9-101 (numerous examples... lies told under oath in his criminal filing petitions, lies about fearing for his life and safety, most recently, lying about obtaining the blog rights)

Good ladies and gentlemen, I am a law-abiding, taxpaying citizen of Maryland and the United States of America. I am homebound and require 24-hour supervision from my wife. Soon, I will progress to the point where I need full time professional care. I will either fall and fatally injure myself or inhale food or liquid, leading to aspiration pneumonia, which will kill me.

I honestly believe this is Mr. Hoge's intent. If you were to file any of these criminal charges against Mr. Hoge, even if I die before the case goes to trial, you could get me under oath on a deposition and that testimony would suffice.

Even if I could find an attorney willing to take my case. I fear I will be dead before discovery, and once I die, so does my case.

I ask you, PLEASE, to give this letter proper consideration. I cannot drive to Carroll County to fill out a citizen charge for the Court Commissioner.

I rely on the law enforcement officials in Carroll County to investigate these allegations of crimes committed within their county, and I rely on the law enforcement officials in Howard County to protect me to the best of their abilities.

Certainly, there can be SOMETHING done to stop Hoge and his relentless, ceaseless, daily attacks against me.

Please, don't wait until I die before you take action.

I appreciate the time you took to read this.

I have difficulty communicating on the telephone, but if you need to call please do.

With all respect,

Bill Schmalfeldt

I thought I was done. I was not. EPWJ was just getting started.
Not happy with attacking me, WJJ Hoge's readership is now attacking the National Parkinson Foundation by publishing the name, phone number and e-mail address of one of their officers. This is because I am donating the proceeds from the sale of my book to the NPF.

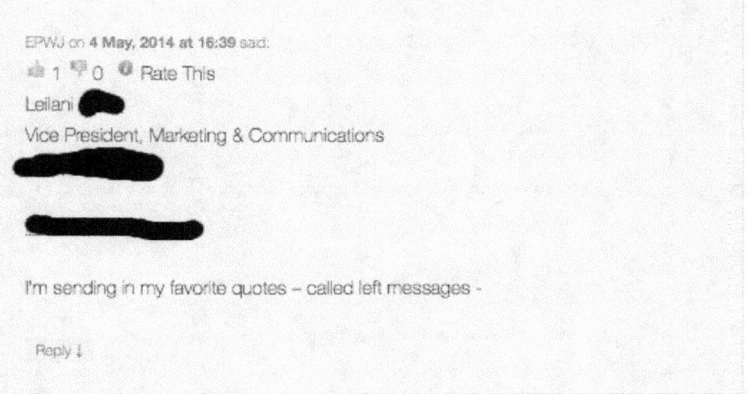

EPWJ on **4 May, 2014 at 16:39** said:

👍 1 👎 0 ⊘ Rate This

Leilani ●●●●

Vice President, Marketing & Communications

I'm sending in my favorite quotes – called left messages –

Reply ↓

This is incredible, inexcusable and another example of the depths to which Hoge and his followers will sink just to harm me.

Why does our law enforcement establishment allow this to continue?

What will it take for someone to take some action.

EPWJ on **4 May, 2014 at 16:54** said:

👍 1 👎 0 ☒ Rate This

Also, out of fairness that Bill is lying and never ever donated one red cent to the NPF, I am alerting the entire management team at the NPF, someone somewhere will tell them, that to ignore these kind of complaints is at their peril, to allow someone who doxes dead babies and live one's who libels people in support of a terrorist – I will plaster this across to all of their major donors, to their public events, to attendees at fundraisers.

They need to take care of this and be aware of it.

all the links you will need are right here

be respectful, and just quote Bill Schmalfeldt – no need for commentary – just were you aware – or FYI – bombard them with the harassment orders, the tweets, the drunken blog posts, etc.

send them reeling into the bathroom to vomit – I know these gentle people will, they seem to be people of conscience, caring people, we will find out, remember he is invoking them. Also I am contacting the NIH, they also have a code of conduct and perhaps his activities can come under some kind of review.

http://www.parkinson.org/About-Us/Our-Team/Senior-Staff

Now, it's not just me they're attacking. They're out to harm an organization that takes care of the 1.5 million Americans with Parkinson's disease and the estimated 60,000 people who will be diagnosed this year.

It's one thing to attack me. But I love the NPF. I love the work they do. And I will be damned if I am going to just sit here while these cretins with no moral compass attack these good people and the good work they do.

As a citizen of Howard County in the State of Maryland, persecuted by a citizen of Carroll County, I demand that action be taken against WJJ Hoge and his readership.

Failure to act will be used as a talking point as the elections approach.

I don't mean to get angry or political, but I don't know what else I can say to get you people to DO SOMETHING!

MY NEXT LETTER WILL BE TO THE BALTIMORE SUN AND THE WASHINGTON POST!!!

Bill Schmalfeldt

It is Sunday night. I have a terrific headache. My eyes do not want to stay in focus. I have had it. I have fought this battle and my allies have fallen away. Meanwhile, Hoge feels strong enough to post this mockery of law enforcement.

UPDATE—

MY NEXT LETTER WILL BE TO THE BALTIMORE SUN AND THE WASHINGTON POST!!!

"Drown me! Roast me! Hang me! Do whatever you please," said Brer Rabbit. "Only please, Brer Fox, please don't throw me into the briar patch."

The thing of it is, he's probably right. In this post Citizen's United, post McCutcheon SCOTUS decision, I no longer have a voice in the government. I have written to everyone who represents Howard County in the state house and senate, the Governor, the Attorney General, Congressman Dutch Ruppersberger, Senator Ben Cardin and Senator Barbara Mikulski.

No response.

If my last name was Soros, someone would talk to me.

But it isn't. So, I have no voice. No voice. No rights.

No reason to fight.

Nobody to fight for.

So, why did I start writing this book?

I don't remember.

However, on May 20, 2014, I decided that I have had just about enough of the abuse.

I filed suit in the US District Court for the District of Maryland (Northern Division). The defendants are...

WJJ Hoge III of Westminster, MD
R. Stacy McCain of Running Waters, WV
Stephen Sheiko of Centerville, VA
Bettina Haper of San Antonio, TX
Nancy Gilly of Groton, CT
Chris Heather of Racine, WI
Kyle Kiernan of South Pasadena, FL
Paul Lemmen of Pinellas Park, FL
Kimberly Dykes of Eastman, GA
The Anonymous Blogger, "Paul Krendler."

The lawsuit awaits a decision from the court as to whether

or not they will allow me to proceed without paying the $400 filing fee. I have confidence that this will be allowed.

The Lickspittle community at Hogewash are outraged that someone as horrid as I would dare stand up for my right to NOT be lied about, libeled, defamed, harassed, have false charges filed against and be intentionally placed under extreme emotional distress.

They defend themselves by bringing up cases in the past where I said something unkind to an anonymous dimwit. They cluck and squawk about filing libel charges against ME, but the problem is… unless I've told a defamatory LIE about a named person, an actual human being, they have no case. Suing me for saying something unkind about "Dee in Texas" is the same as suing me for calling "The Lone Ranger" a coward. They are both fictional characters. When you choose to hide behind the mask of anonymity, you lose the right to legal recourse when someone attacks you.

I am sure the judge will rule in my favor on the pauper filing.

I am even more sure that if the case makes it in front of a jury, I will prevail.

EPILOGUE

He gazed up at the enormous face. Forty years it had taken him to learn what kind of smile was hidden beneath the dark moustache. O cruel, needless misunderstanding! O stubborn, self-willed exile from the loving breast! Two gin-scented tears trickled down the sides of his nose. But it was all right, everything was all right, the struggle was finished. He had won the victory over himself. He loved Big Brother.

Last paragraph of "1984" by George Orwell
© 1981 Rosenblum Productions, Inc
Used under Fair Use Terms of US Copyright Law
(Unless WJJ Hoge bought the rights and we haven't been told.)

ABOUT THE AUTHOR

I'm retired from my job as a writer/editor with the federal government after dealing with Parkinson's disease for more than 14 years. I keep myself busy by writing, blogging at http://patriot-ombusman.com, running an online radio station at http://brainslices.com, and my new hobby is suing the reprobates and their lickspittle lackeys who have destroyed my online reputation.

BILL SCHMALFELDT